TRAINING FOR CHANGES IN I.T.

ISBN: 978-1-326-14325-1

TRAINING FOR CHANGES IN I.T.

ISBN: 978-1-326-14325-1

CONTENTS **Page**

SECTION ONE

1. MANAGEMENT OF CHANGE

1.1 CONCEPT

Change Management and the changes to Configuration, Release, and Assets as a whole group of activities have traditionally been concerned with finding effective solutions to specific operational problems. The purpose of this book is to look at current problems and new, better methods, techniques, and tools for processing changes.

In the past, it has been found that too many of the solutions are not implemented and, of those that are, too few survive the inclination of client functional areas to return to familiar ways of doing things.

Therefore, Change Management personnel have gradually come to realize that their tasks should not only include solving specific problems but also designing problem-solving and implementation systems that predict and prevent future problems, identify and solve current ones, and implement and maintain these solutions under changing conditions.

As an Executive in multi-national organisations and Government Departments, the author has come to realise that most problems do not arise in isolation but are part of an interacting system. Thus the book, in principle, is seeking for a process of simultaneous interrelated solutions to a set of interdependent problems. Further more, substantial effort has been devoted in recommending a rational methodology for one, or the least possible processes, for future change management.

Businesses need to find better ways of doing things, is often not nearly as great as is the need to maximize use of what is already operational. This book, therefore, has been addressing itself more and more to determining how to produce the willingness to change procedures suitable to the way people are willing to work and with processes that they are familiar with.

The book, which follows various consultancy assignments, considers the additional, more detailed recommendations, including strategic changes, training, convincing resources, meetings with people, development of workshops and exchanges of new ideas. The reader, therefore, must consider such points that absorb resources, excessive costs and incur a heavy workload for existing staff.

In the areas in which technology advances fastest, new products and new materials are required in a constant flow, but there are many client areas in which the rate of change can be gentle. Although each process considered may be trivial, the total effect is many times as large as the margin between success and failure in an operational situation. These efforts to improve existing processes have been formalised under the various sections of this book.

The legacy processes and their procedures have had a dramatic impact on the management of changes. The speed and data-handling capabilities of experienced staff, enables the realistic changes and because of their know-how they get meaningful solutions to those changes through the use of long standing techniques.

The changes occurring under such circumstances consist of calculating the performance of a system by evaluating a model of it for randomly selected values of variables contained within a unique process and its procedures. Most changes under such operations are concerned with "stochastic" variables; that is, variables whose values change randomly within some probability distribution over time.

There is still considerable difficulty, however, in drawing inferences from operational legacy processes to the real world of smooth Change Management. Additionally, the growing number of changes in the information-processing applications is currently on the increase. To this effect, the recommendations made in this book may be the optimum solution to the problems of adopting new processes.

The procedures recommended as processes, will improve the cost-effectiveness of changes and their management. In the realm of the economy, they may be expected to lead to higher productivity, particularly in the service sectors and related processes, decision-making, problem solving, administration, and support of clerical functions.

Awareness that possession of information on any changes is tantamount to a competitive edge is stimulating the gathering of information at national levels. Similarly, concern is mounting over the safeguarding and husbanding of changes to the proprietary and strategic information within the confines of a client, as well as within outsourcing companies. Administration-oriented information systems and the management of changes in client sites have as their objective the husbanding and optimisation of corporate resources, namely; employees and their activities, inventories of materials and equipment, facilities, and finances.

A client's administrative information systems and the Management Information Systems (MIS) focus primarily on resource administration and provide top management with reports of aggregate data. Executive information systems may be viewed as an evolution of administrative information systems in the direction of strategic tracking, modelling, and decision-making. Typically, Change Management consists of a number of processes, each supporting a particular function and changes, which may occur any day of the year.

Change Management processes concentrate on resource allocation and task completion of organised activities. They usually incorporate such scheduling methods as the Critical Path Method (CPM) or Program Evaluation and Review Technique (PERT).

The processes, with which the book is concerned, are first of all man-made. Second, some of them are small and simple to manage, or they are large and complex, depending on the changes required. Their component parts sometimes interact so extensively that a change in one part is likely to affect many others.

It is, therefore, of primary importance that all the Change Management processes interact with all the functionalities. Otherwise, Change Management as a tool is of no significance. Processes may also vary depending on the amount of human judgment that enters into their operation.

1.2 Programme Management

Programme Management may have many responsibilities, but the most important of all is the ability to identify and positively execute plans to manage the changes threatening the objectives.

Through a process of structured interviews and plans the Assessment Analysis is used to highlight the specific requests for changes, which may turn into risks. During the interviews Assessment Analysis is used to capture the key changes from the interviewees.

In turn, the Assessment Analysis provides a life-cycle process, which highlights the primary prioritisation of the changes. In large, complex, and critical programmes, it is essential that a true prioritised report is available so that the imminent changes can be managed first.

The process commences by identifying the most important changes, which may become threats to a project. These are given priority, support and management expertise. Once the prioritisation exercise is completed, the participating people are notified and subsequently interviewed to bring out and capture any possible changes they may have.

Within a programme, projects are prioritised to ensure that those most critical to the programme's success are given priority to scarce resources.

1.3 Methodology

The Management of Change allows the capture of collective knowledge and expertise from those involved on the project, in a form that facilitates the communication of changes, their assessments, and the pro-active management of the changes requested.

In essence, this is the mechanism by which the functions of Information Technology programmes and projects are held together as a result of the principles operating within the methodology for the management of change, as in the S:I:G:M:A: paragraphs below:

- **Systematic: The varied Changes, their Assessments, and the consequential Risks relating to or consisting of a system.**

Methodical in procedures and plans, these are addressed to those involved and deliberating within the parameters of their systems development responsibilities.

- **Integration: The results being dependable on the mutual or reciprocal action which encourages those involved in the programmes and projects to communicate with each other and to work closely with a view to solving the threatening changes before they impact on the development of the system.**

- **Generic: The individuals involved maintain an approach, which relates and characterises the whole group of those involved in assessing the changes and attacking any threatening ones before they become risks to the development of the system. The end result being the avoidance of apparent problems within the pre-defined users' systems requirements.**

- **Methodology: Following the system architects and the change management practitioners enable this. Simply follow the approved body of systems development methods, rules and management procedures employed by their organisation. For practical or even ethical reasons, it must be noted that with such a philosophy, it is seldom possible to fulfil all requirements of very large organisational systems.**

- **Applications: As such, Change Management is administered by putting to use such techniques and in applying the Change Management principles in the development of various applications will involve numerous and varied activities.**

A concrete issue in developing new applications is the problem of communication among the people involved, the motivation constantly needed for generic work, the ability to interact systematically and in using Change Management.

2. I.T. PROGRAMS AND CHANGE MANAGEMENT

2.1 Substitution of Conditions

In general, the Management of Change, deals with the substitution of one thing or set of conditions for another, thus making something different from its previous condition, be it an alteration in state or quality, variety, variation, mutation.

More specific, in the Information Technology environment anything that becomes different, be it the performance of a system, the planning of new enhancements, the development of new systems and their various phases, the complete configuration and its assets, releases, all this require a structure approach.

Change Management in Information Technology Programmes Management, therefore, includes and enables any:

- **Alteration,**
- **Modification,**
- **Conversion,**
- **Variance,**
- **Transformation,**
- **Remodelling,**
- **Reconstruction,**
- **Re-organization,**
- **Substitution,**
- **Replacement.**

Any kind or type of change which may occur and affect a systems configuration, releases, and assets, be it hardware, software or whatever the term of Information Technology may represent.

This process spans the whole life cycle from initial concept and definition of business needs through to the end of the useful life of an asset or end of a services contract. Both conventionally funded and more innovative types of funded projects are included.

This definition is consistent with modern supply chain management practices. The process is not limited to the purchasing function in companies and departments and is inherently multi-functional especially in large, complex, and/or novel procurements.

2.2 Leader for Change Management

The Change Management Leader proposes and agrees the scope of:

- **The Change Management processes, function, the items that are to be controlled, and the information that is to be recorded,**
- **Develops Change Management standards, Change Management plans, and procedures,**
- **Evaluates Change Management tools and recommends those that best meet the organisation's budget, resource, timescale, and technical requirements,**
- **Creates and manages the Change Management plan,**
- **Performs audits to check that the physical Information Technology inventory is consistent with the Change Management Database, and**
- **Initiates the actions needed to secure funds to enhance the infrastructure and staffing levels in order to cope with growth and change.**

3. CYCLE

3.1 Request, Assessment, Change, and Register

The concept being a simple one as shown in the diagram below:

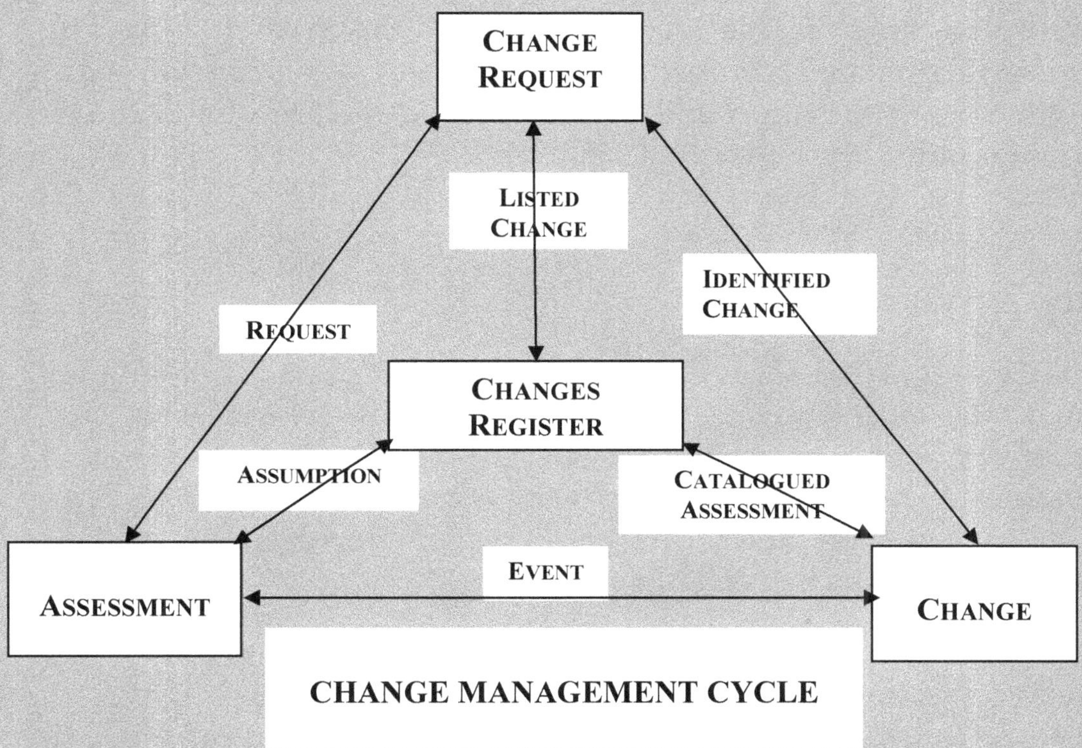

CHANGE MANAGEMENT CYCLE

The Change Management principles explained in this book were developed by the author whilst employed by *PsySys Limited,* over a period of twenty-four years. The methodology was used for PsySys' international clients, from 1980 onwards. The idea of a structured approached to organisational requests for changes and their management proved beneficial to customers and users who integrated the full process with other methodologies, such as Structured Systems Analysis and Designing methods and Project Management procedures.

3.2 Managing the Change Programme

It is basic business sense to identify, assess, manage, and monitor changes that are significant to the fulfilment of an organisation's business objectives. In recent years businesses have been transformed by, and are in many cases heavily dependent on I.T.

The financial consequences of a breakdown in controls or a security breach are not only the loss incurred, but also the costs of recovering and preventing further failures. The impact is not only financial: it can affect adversely reputation and brand value as well as the business' performance and future potential.

3.3 Impact on Business

Boards can regard inadequate system development as a significant risk, and where directors feel that this may be the situation in their organisations, they may need to ask tough questions of themselves and their management teams. Systems development and their changes is an issue that boards may need to recognise should regularly be on their agenda, and not delegated to I.T. technicians.

Business in the past was primarily confined to assessment of the change and its associated risk surrounding fire, flood, and Acts of God. In business today we have become high dependent on information systems.

Failure to build computer systems as required and the changes requested thereafter, by the users has a major impact on our business to function. The inability of companies to provide adequate systems can cause potential problems to customers, suppliers, employees and an all round havoc to information.

3.4 STAFF TRAINING

One of the greatest threats in Change Management is the non-acceptance of it or misuse of the system by the organisation's own personnel. Obtaining their buy-in is essential. It is obvious that someone is going to be appointed to ensure that the change management principles are adhered to and the system maintained throughout the organisation.

It is, also, important that if information leaves the organisation by its transference to others for use on the company's behalf, that they have adequate systems to protect the set standards.

The successful implementation of Change Management is reliant upon people and in particular the employees whose contracts of employment may need adjustment to protect the company and the adequate management and execution of plans for the solution to the threats caused by the changes identified.

4. ANALYSES

4.1 Assessment of Changes

Fundamental to the creation of a Change Management system is the assessment of the changes (Changes Analysis) to your business and the potential loss that could accrue if things go wrong. Change Assessment software tools are available in the market, which can be used by consultants, or by internal staff. What is important is the ability to assess the change to your business and the cost to protect it against the change. The end result is that you have to make the valued judgement on the amount the business spends, on the implementation and the monitoring of a change policy.

Products and systems are available to counter the threats and changes that have been identified. There is a wide range of options available, but remember that anything chosen will require expertise to design and complete a system, taking into account how the various solutions will inter-react with each other. Like all things to do with I.T., the design and implementation of systems, change solutions are only as good as the people installing them.

4.2 Communication

The most important factor in the success of any management style is the ability to communicate with each other, one to one or in groups of people. The art of communication is just as important to the whole process of the management of changes. More so, where the changes identified have become a threat because of the problem of human communications.

This is where the appointment of an experienced and trained Change Practitioner is worth the effort put into securing such individual/s.

4.3 Practice

A trained Change Management Practitioner will have enough knowledge to run and maintain the system, as well as ample experience to be able to communicate with all levels of employees, hold meetings, and ensure the plans executed.

In brief and as the diagram on the next page shows (Section Two – 5. Training), the Practitioner will be responsible for the complete Change Management cycle.

SECTION TWO

5. TRAINING

About 120 slides in jpeg are included in this section. For the purpose of self-training, it is recommended that the reader follows these pictures diligently.

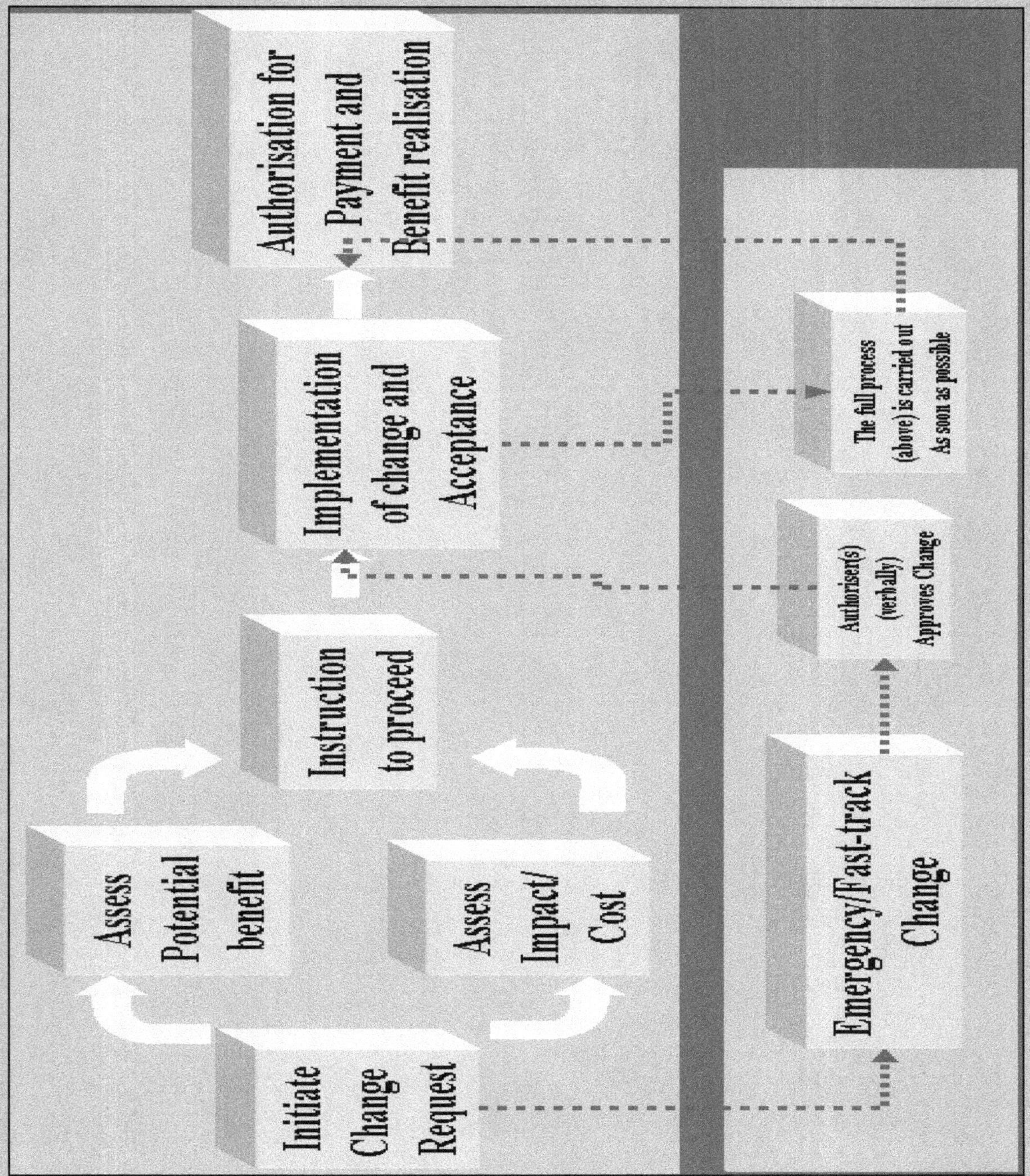

Change Management In I.T.
Practitioner Training

Objectives of the Change Management Roll-out

The training aims to establish four levels of "expertise" within an organisation

•Awareness – understands the basics of Assumption Analysis, how it works and how it is implemented.

•Practitioner – Awareness plus competent Assumption Analysis interviewer.

•Expert – Practitioner plus able to set-up and support new implementations

Trainer – Expert plus able to train to Practitioner level

A.T. Kearney 12/Document / 22/12/2014

Course content

- Introduction
  - Traditional change management techniques
    - Principles of project change management
    - Theory vs practice
- Programme/project change management
  - Change identification and analysis
  - Change prioritisation
  - Change control
  - Project Prioritisation – Programme Change Management
  - Conclusions
- Workshop - Assumption Analysis Interviewing techniques

A.T. Kearney 12/Document / 22/[illegible]

Introduction
What is a project ?

Introduction
What is a project and what do we mean by "change" ?
Project:
• Something complex that you want (plan) to happen

Introduction

What is a project and what do we mean by "change" ?

- Project:
  - Something complex that you want (plan) to happen

- Change:
  - Something that you want to happen

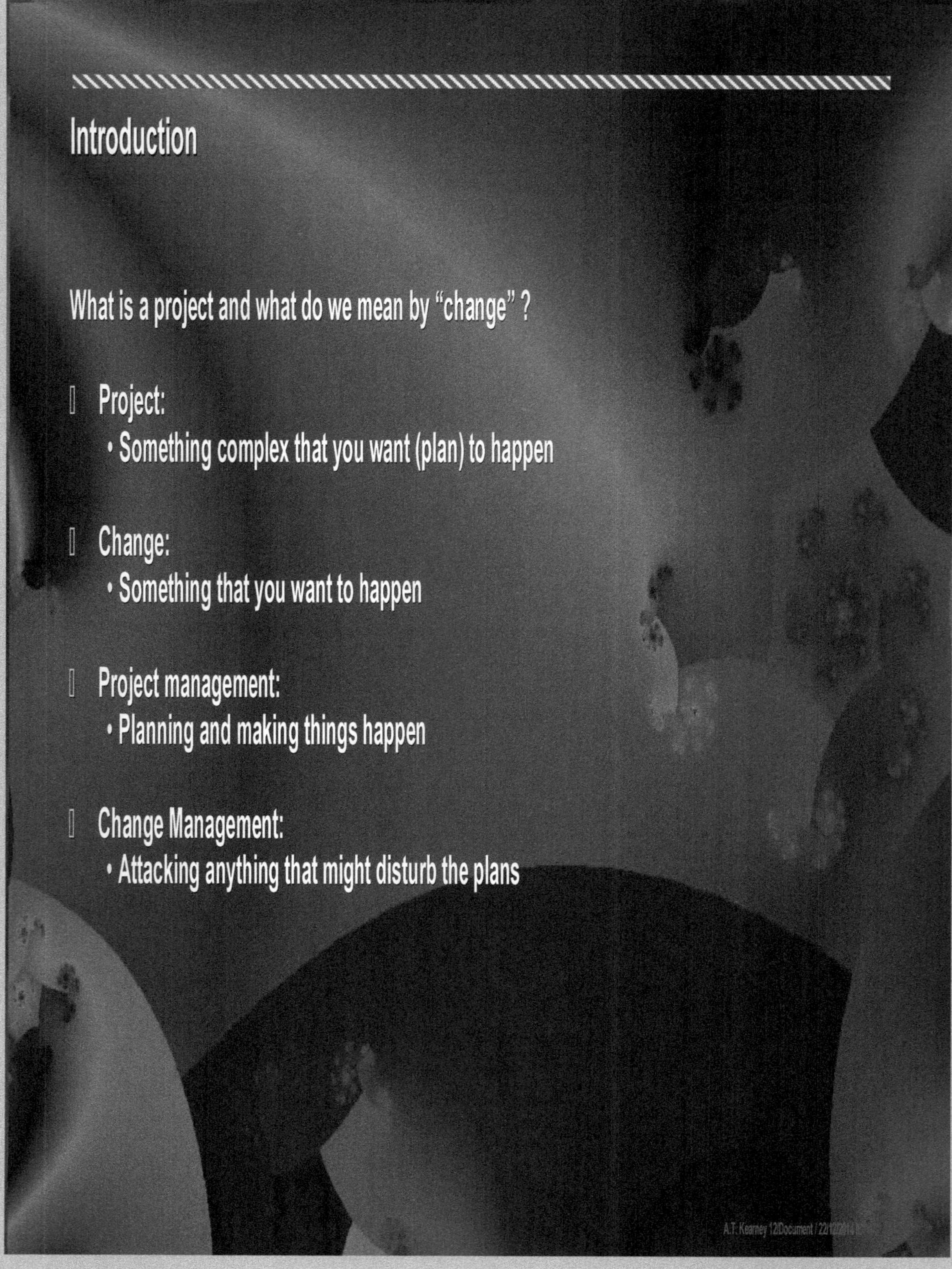
Introduction
What is a project and what do we mean by "change" ?
Project:
• Something complex that you want (plan) to happen
Change:
• Something that you want to happen
Project management:
• Planning and making things happen
Change Management:
• Attacking anything that might disturb the plans

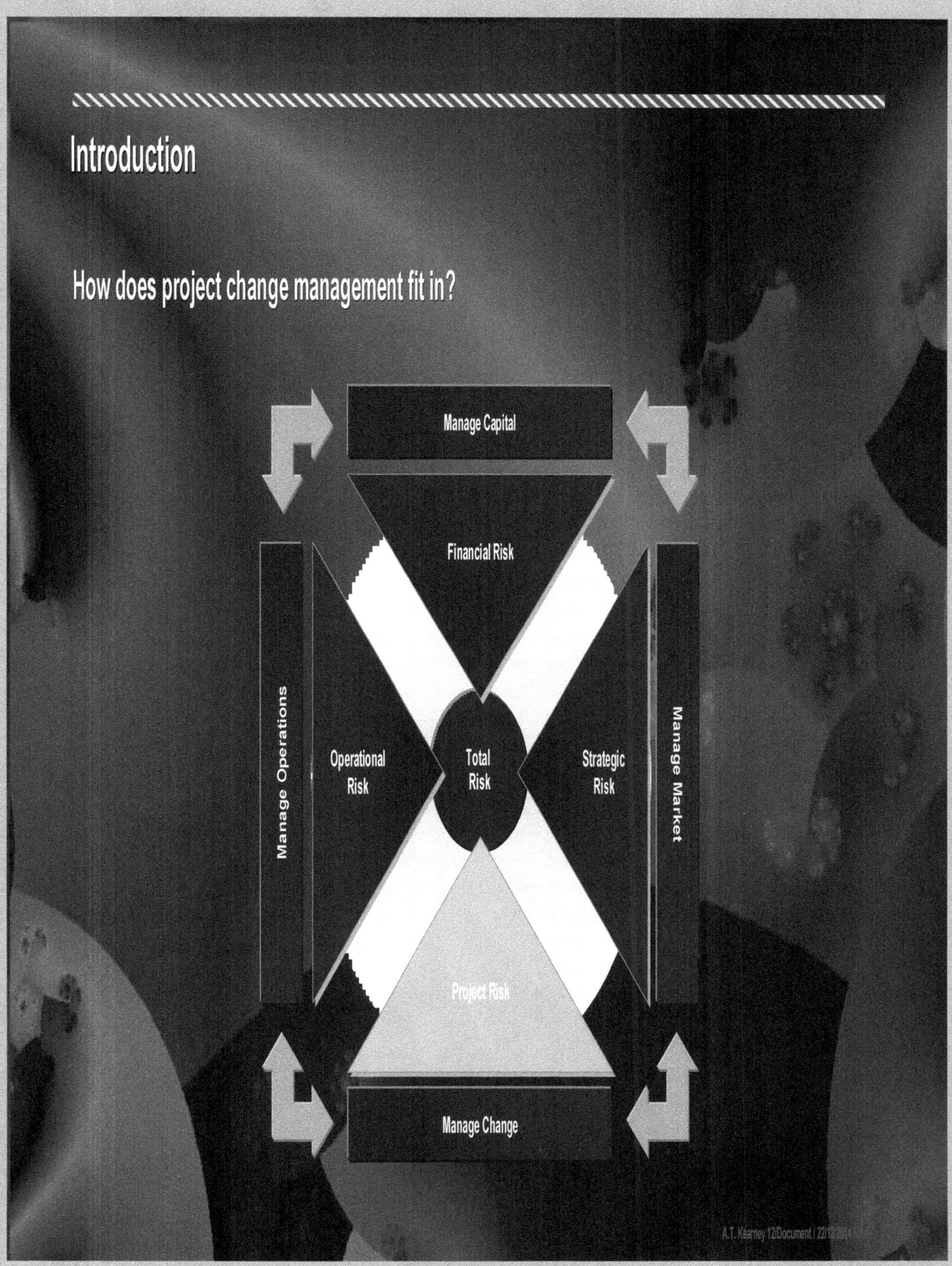
Introduction
How does project change management fit in?
Manage Capital
Financial Risk
Manage Operations
Operational Risk
Total Risk
Strategic Risk
Manage Market
Project Risk
Manage Change

Introduction
If its such a great idea, why is formal change management rarely applied ?

Introduction

If its such a great idea, why is formal change management rarely applied ?

- Unwillingness to admit that changes are needed
- "Just do it" culture

A.T. Kearney 12/Document / 22/12/2014 ID 10

Introduction
If its such a great idea, why is formal change management rarely applied ?
Unwillingness to admit that changes are needed
"Just do it" culture
Natural tendency to focus on the easy parts of the project

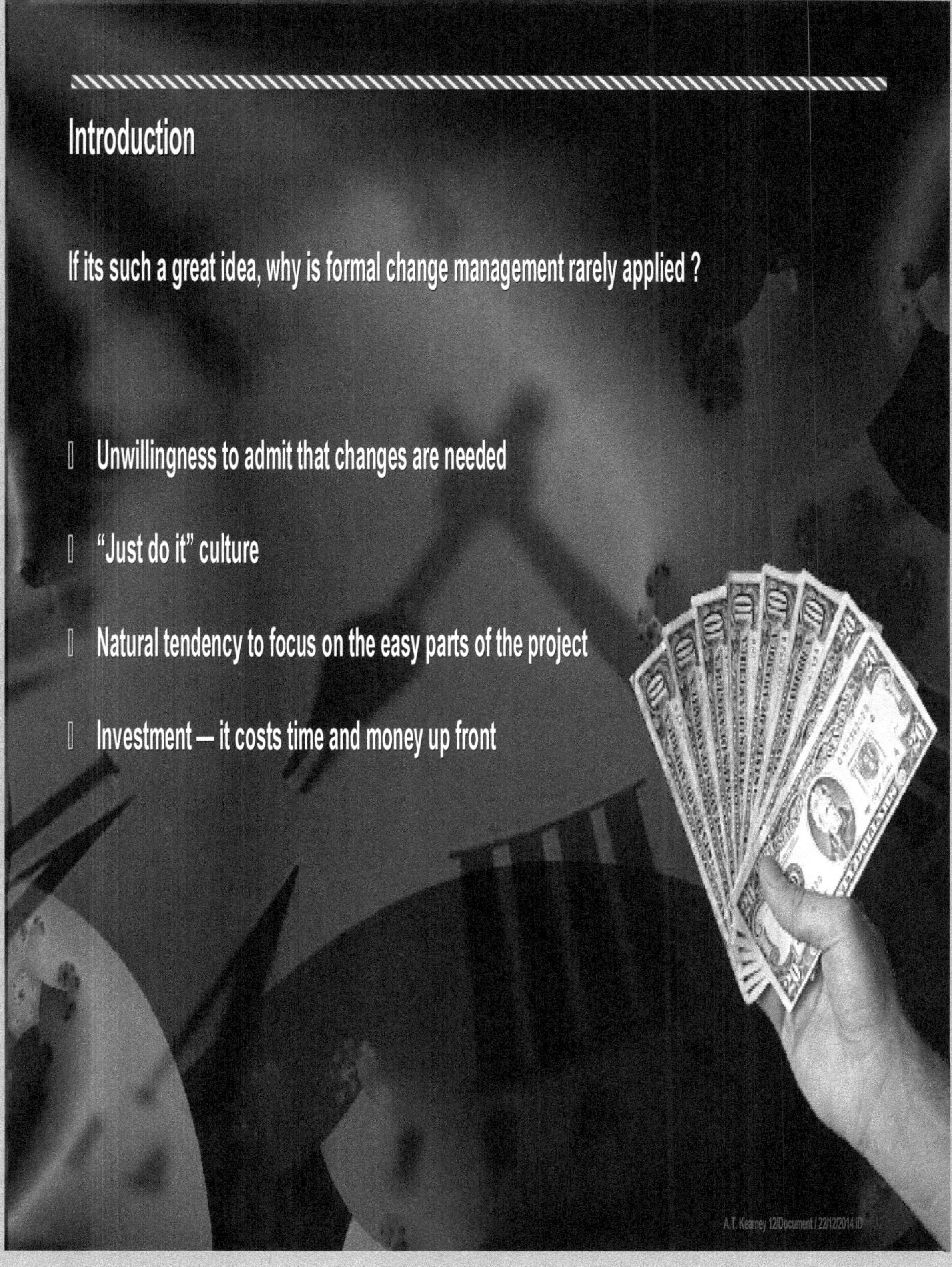
Introduction
If its such a great idea, why is formal change management rarely applied ?
Unwillingness to admit that changes are needed
"Just do it" culture
Natural tendency to focus on the easy parts of the project
Investment – it costs time and money up front

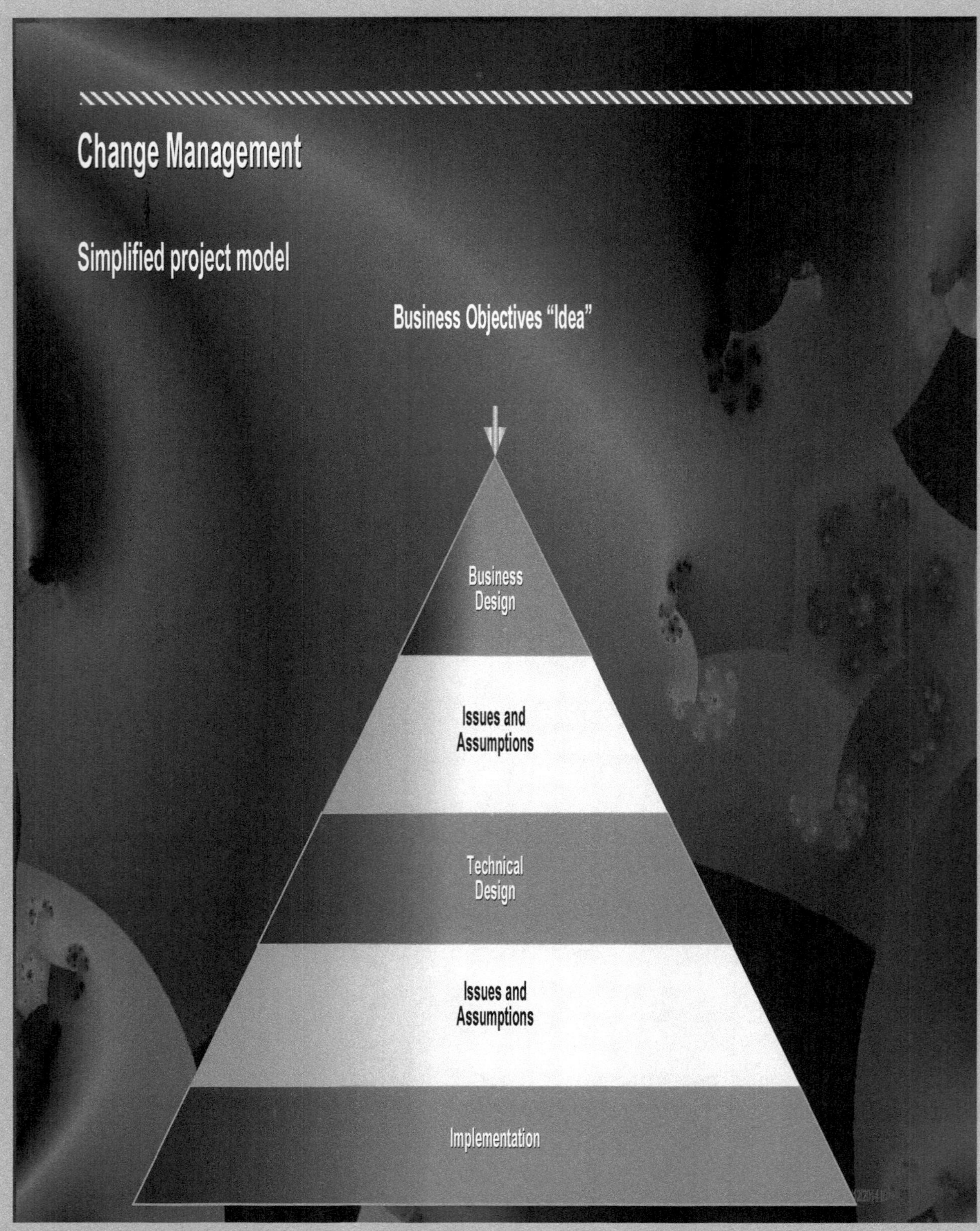
Change Management
Simplified project model
Business Objectives "Idea"
Business Design
Issues and Assumptions
Technical Design
Issues and Assumptions
Implementation

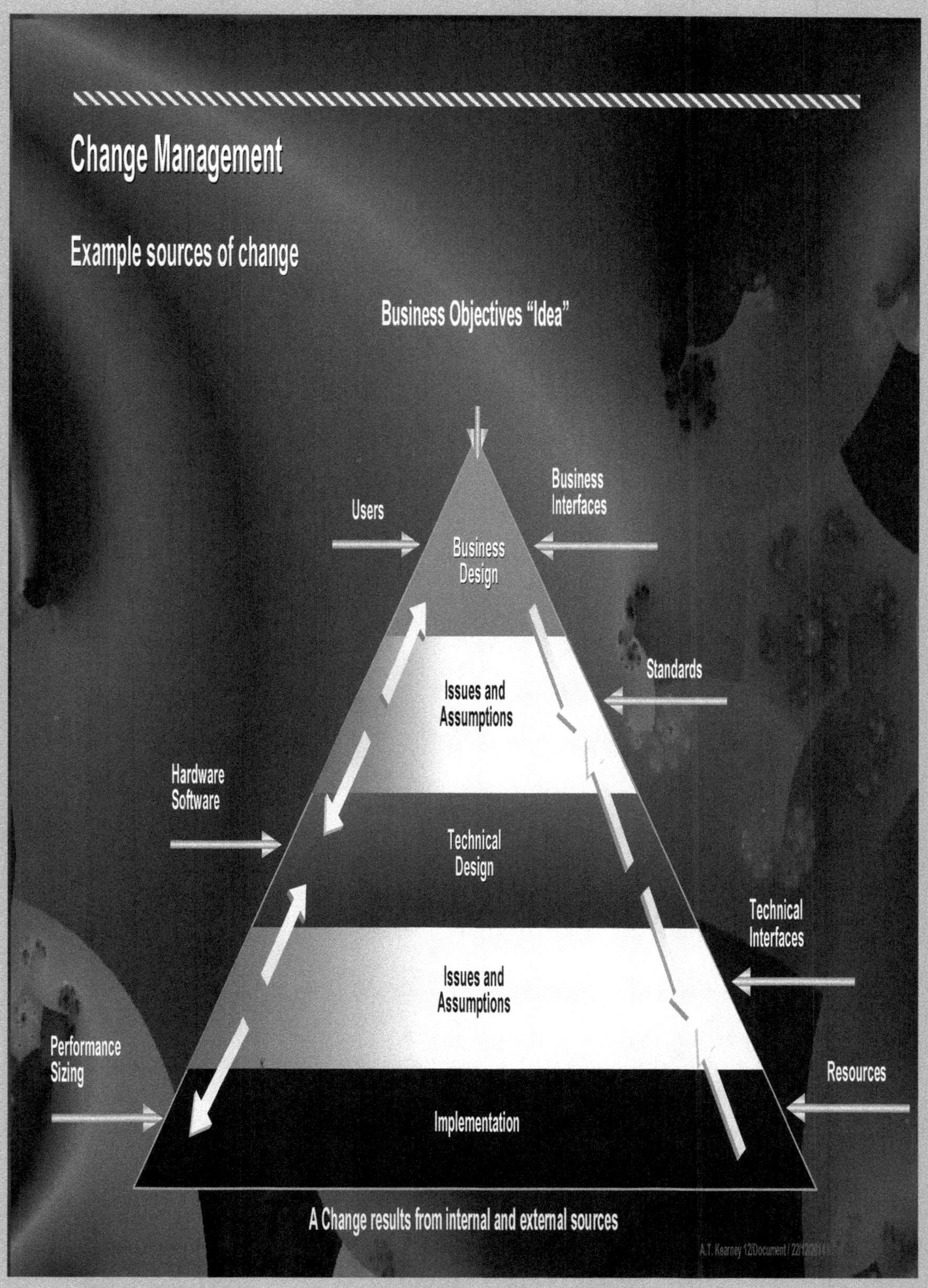
Change Management
Example sources of change
Business Objectives "Idea"
Users
Business Interfaces
Business Design
Issues and Assumptions
Standards
Hardware Software
Technical Design
Technical Interfaces
Issues and Assumptions
Performance Sizing
Resources
Implementation
A Change results from internal and external sources
A.T. Kearney 12/Document /

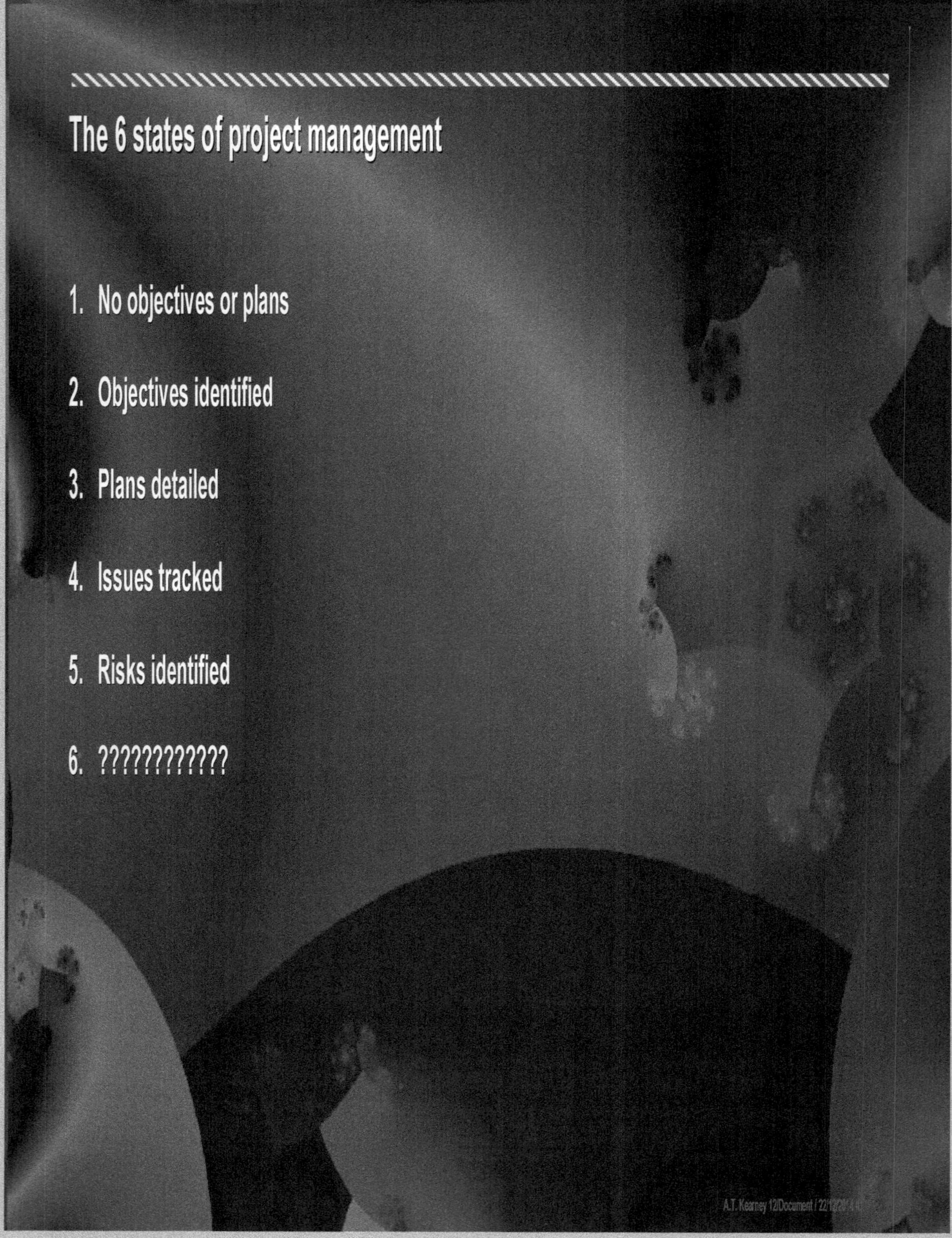
The 6 states of project management
1. No objectives or plans
2. Objectives identified
3. Plans detailed
4. Issues tracked
5. Risks identified
6. ????????????

Traditional Change
Management Techniques

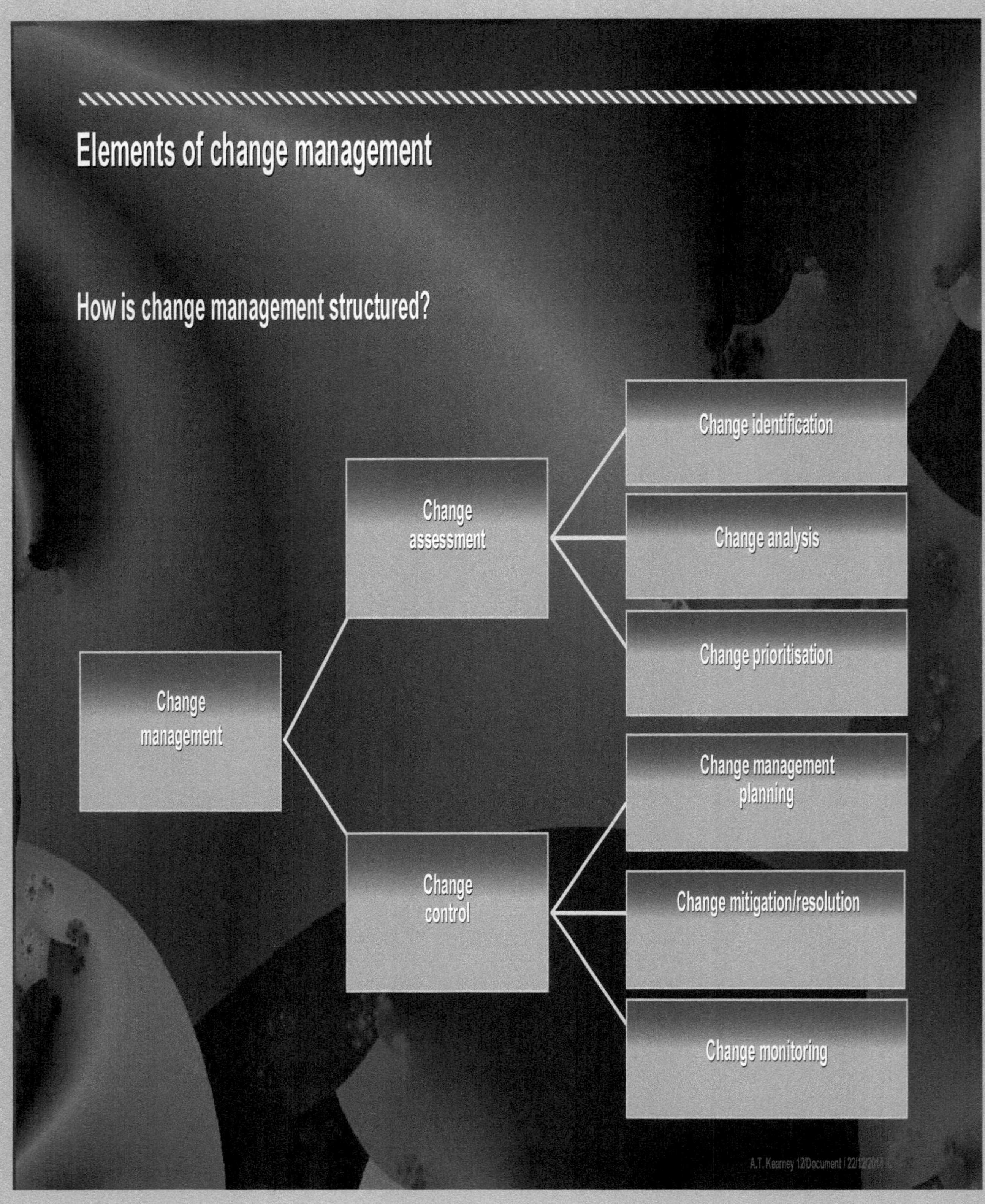
Elements of change management
How is change management structured?
Change management
Change assessment
Change control
Change identification
Change analysis
Change prioritisation
Change management planning
Change mitigation/resolution
Change monitoring
A.T. Kearney 12/Document /

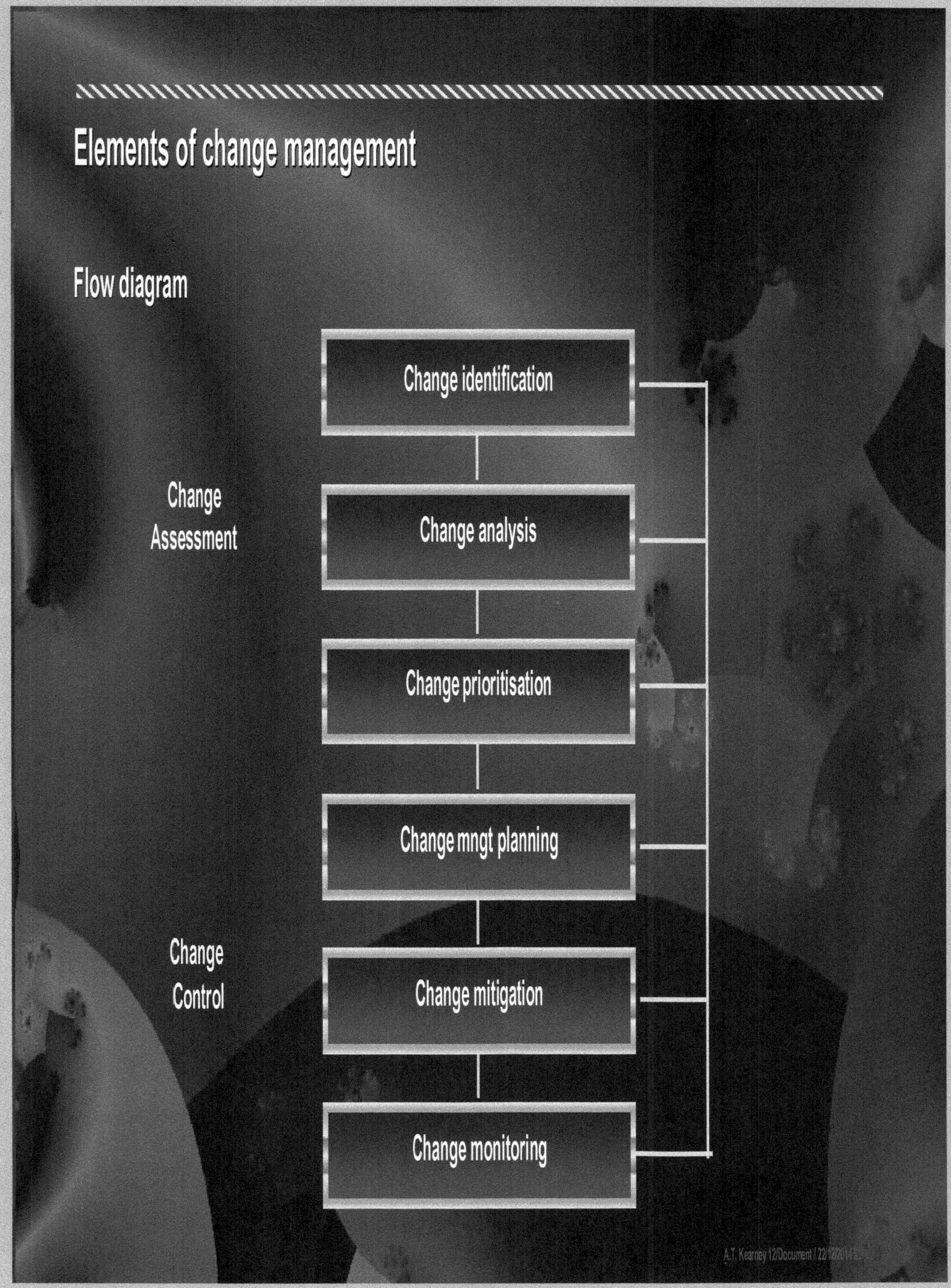
Elements of change management
Flow diagram
Change Assessment
Change Control
Change identification
Change analysis
Change prioritisation
Change mngt planning
Change mitigation
Change monitoring

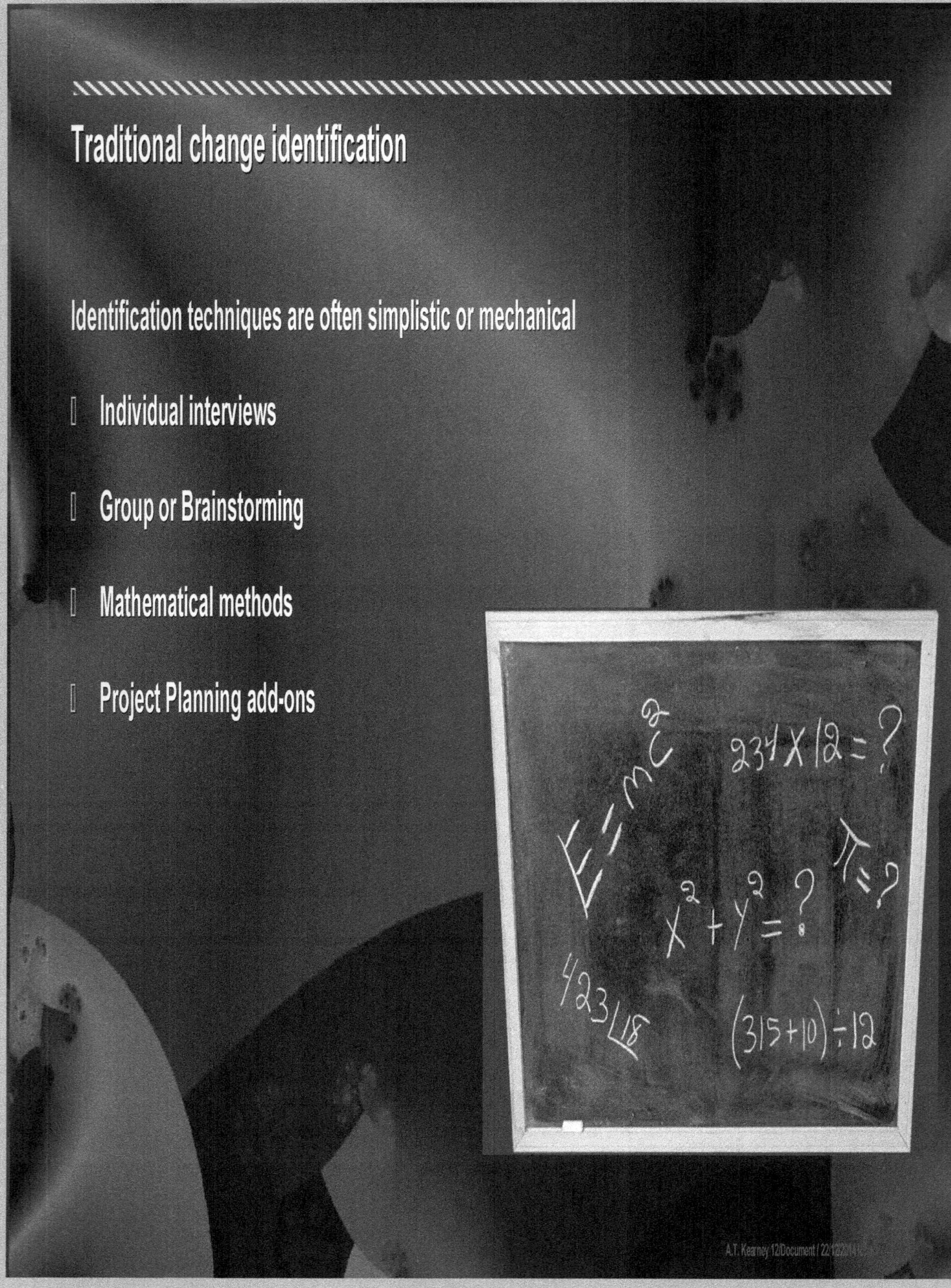
Traditional change identification
Identification techniques are often simplistic or mechanical
Individual interviews
Group or Brainstorming
Mathematical methods
Project Planning add-ons
E = mc2
234 X 12 = ?
x2 + y2 = ?
π = ?
(315+10) ÷ 12

Traditional change management

Change management responsibilities are often inefficient and confusing

- Change Owners are normally appointed who are responsible for the management of the change
- A Change Manager is tasked with driving the process
- The Project Manager often owns many of the changes
- Any change action plans are normally simple and informal

A.T. Kearney 12/Document / 22/[illegible]

Traditional change management
Approach to Change Action Planning
Fall-back plans rather than pro-active
Concentration on change transfer
Strategies rather than specifics

Traditional change management

Conclusion

- Traditional change management techniques can yield significant benefits but often do not due to:
  - Failing to get to the specifics
  - Analysis based on poor quality data
  - Lack of ownership
  - Seen as an administrative overhead
  - Failure to handle personal or political bias

A.T. Kearney 12/Document / 22/12/201

Programme/Project
Change
Management
A.T. Kearney 12/Document / 22/12/2014

Content

- Change identification and analysis
  - Assumption analysis
  - Strategic cost analysis ("Brick") analysis
  - Work plan analysis
- Change prioritisation ("Bubble Diagrams")
- Change control
  - Action plans ("Attacking Change s")
  - Management structures
  - Admin support and reporting
- Project Prioritisation (Complexity/Criticality Diagrams)
- Workshop - Assumption Analysis Interviewing techniques

A.T. Kearney 12/Document /

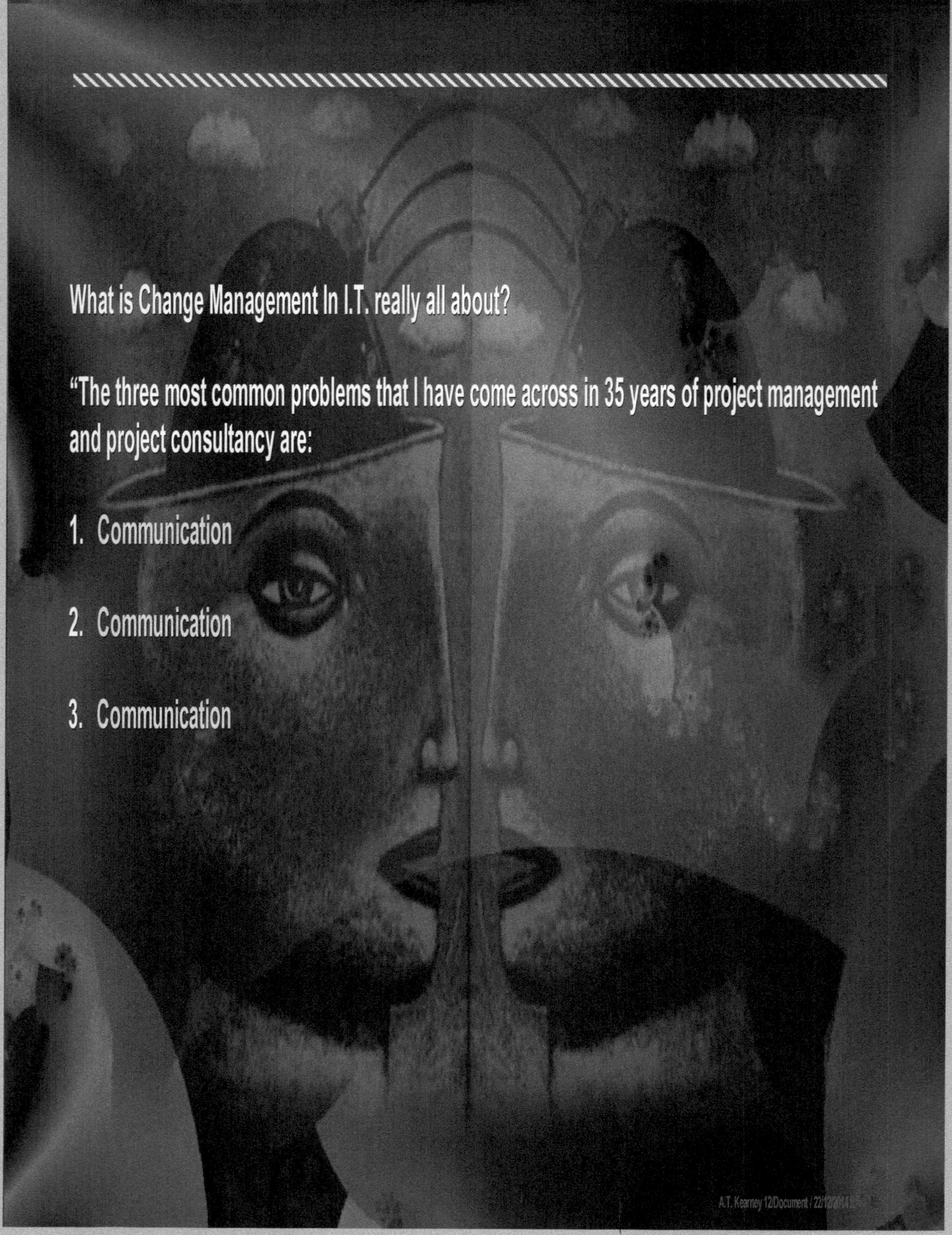
What is Change Management In I.T. really all about?
"The three most common problems that I have come across in 35 years of project management and project consultancy are:
1. Communication
2. Communication
3. Communication
A.T. Kearney 12/Document /

Change Management In I.T.

What needs to be communicated?

- Firstly, all significant business change initiatives can and should be run as fully planned projects or programs
- Projects only fail due to three fundamental reasons:
  - The assumptions we make go wrong
  - We incorrectly assess the significance of the assumptions we make
  - We fail to communicate the assumptions that we make
- Therefore the capture, analysis and communication of these assumptions is critical to the success of any project and, ultimately, the business

A.T. Kearney 12/Document / 22/1

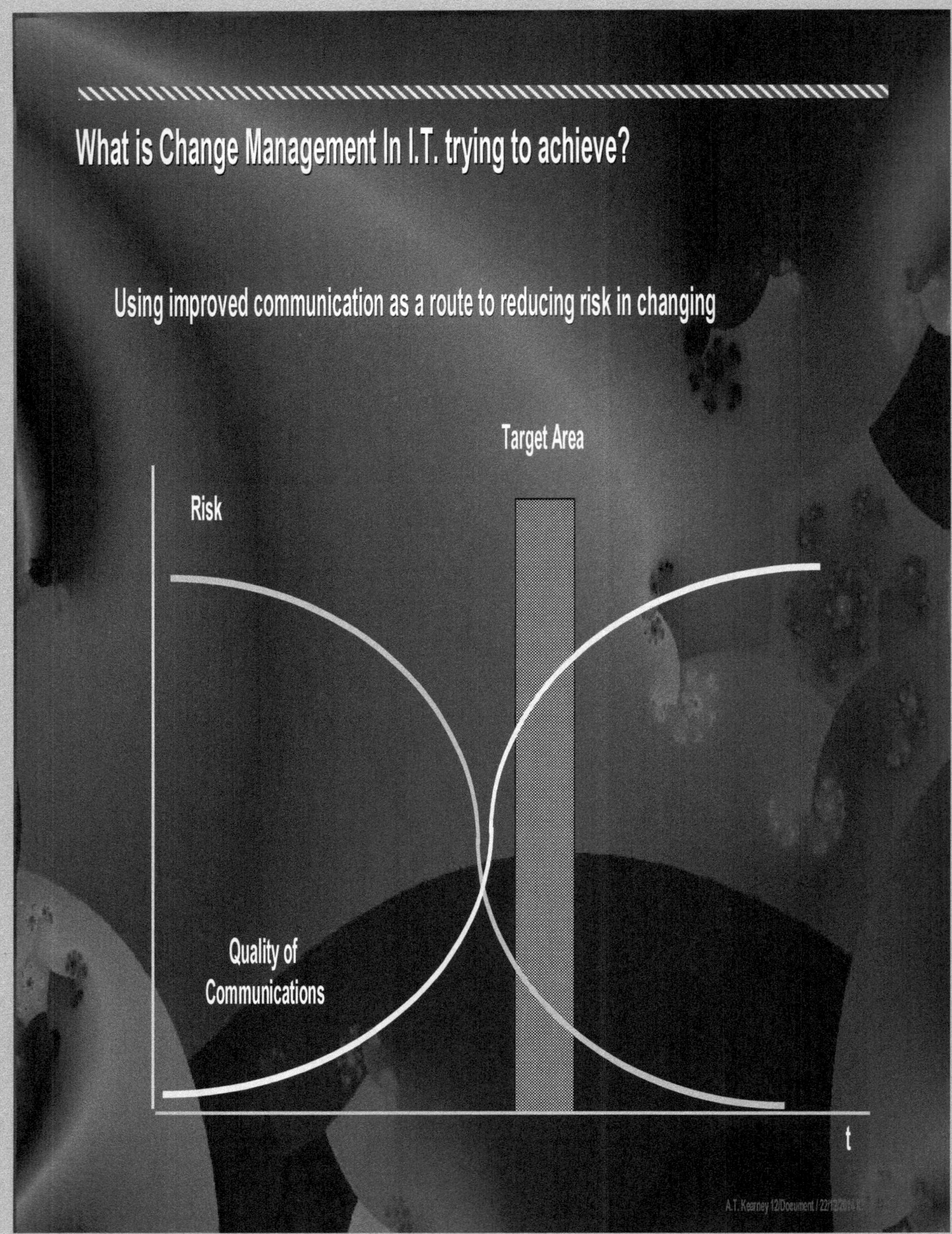
What is Change Management In I.T. trying to achieve?
Using improved communication as a route to reducing risk in changing
Target Area
Risk
Quality of
Communications
t
A.T. Kearney 12/Document

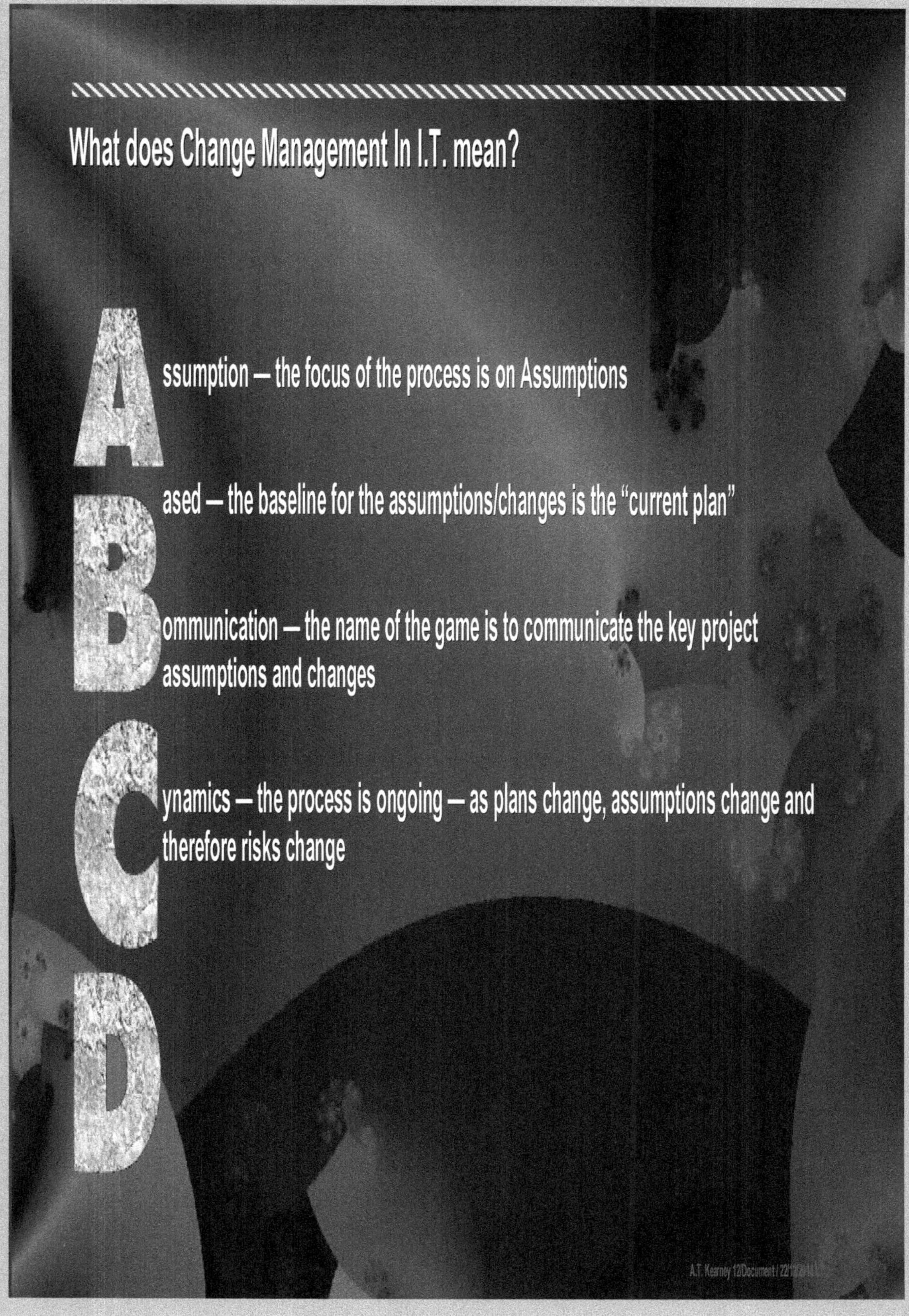
What does Change Management In I.T. mean?
A
ssumption – the focus of the process is on Assumptions
B
ased – the baseline for the assumptions/changes is the "current plan"
C
ommunication – the name of the game is to communicate the key project assumptions and changes
D
ynamics – the process is ongoing – as plans change, assumptions change and therefore risks change

ABCD Ratings
The ABCD Scale
A
B
C
D
Desirable
Good
Low Priority
High Quality
No Problem
Undesirable
Bad
High Priority
Poor Quality
Big Problem

How was Change Management In I.T. developed?

- Major change programme in trouble
- Extensive study of commercial change management methods and tools
- Evaluation of "what works well in practice and why?"
- What makes projects 'tick'?
- Development of new techniques to "plug the gaps"
- Development of method based on use

A.T. Kearney 12/Document / 22/[illegible]

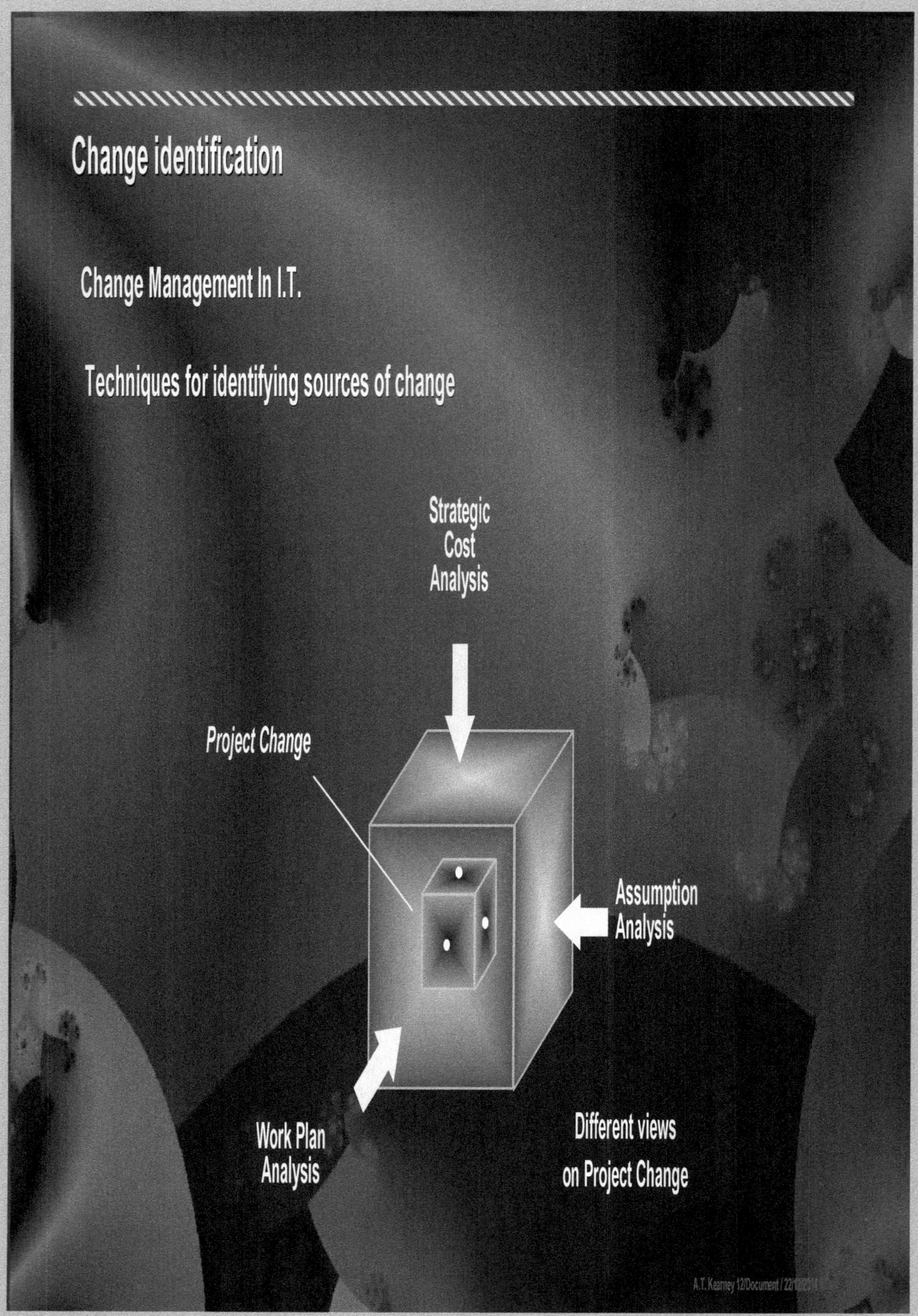
Change identification
Change Management In I.T.
Techniques for identifying sources of change
Strategic Cost Analysis
Project Change
Assumption Analysis
Work Plan Analysis
Different views on Project Change

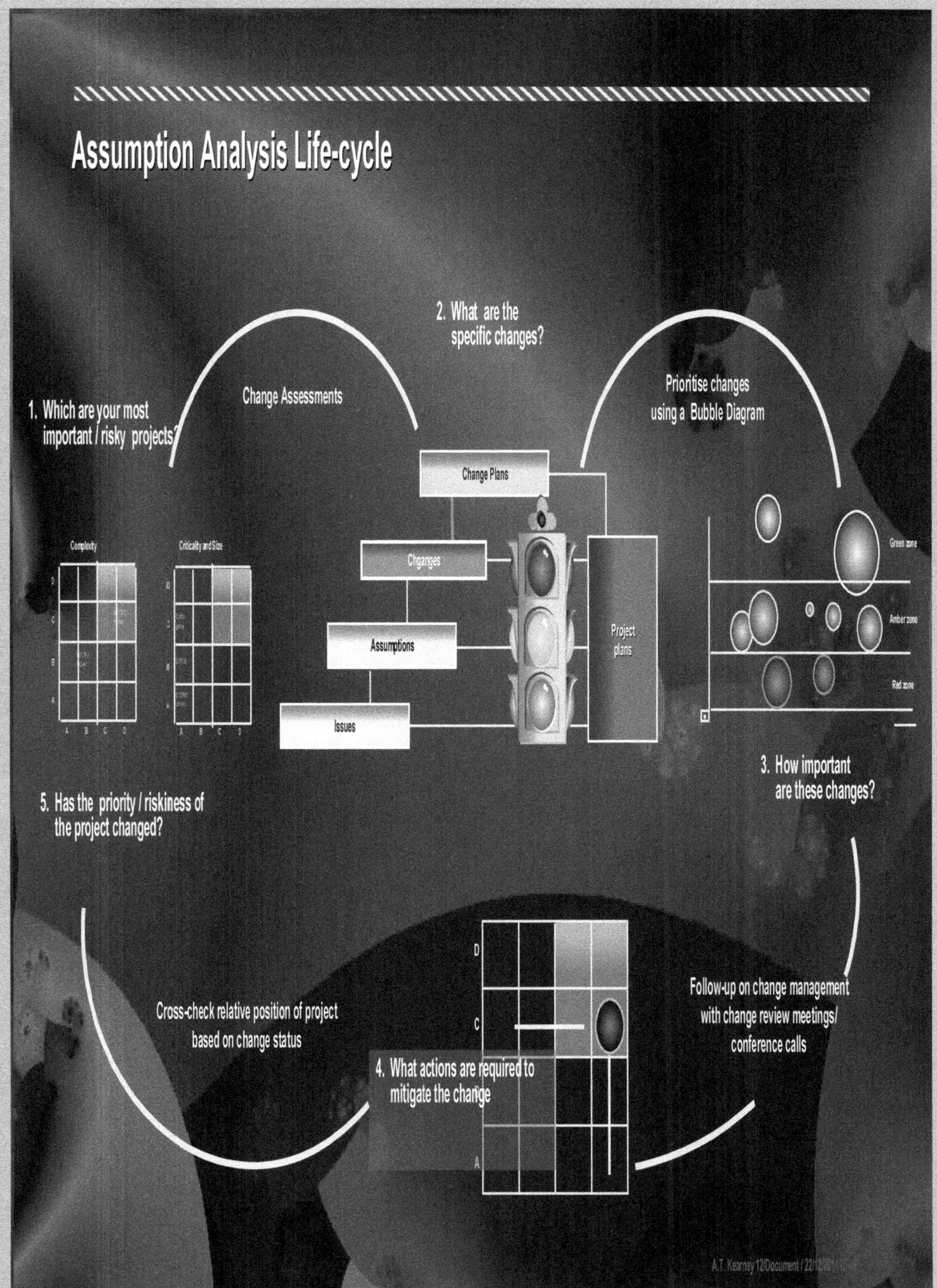
Assumption Analysis Life-cycle
1. Which are your most important / risky projects?
Change Assessments
2. What are the specific changes?
Prioritise changes using a Bubble Diagram
Change Plans
Chganges
Assumptions
Issues
Project plans
Complexity
Criticality and Size
Green zone
Amber zone
Red zone
3. How important are these changes?
5. Has the priority / riskiness of the project changed?
Cross-check relative position of project based on change status
4. What actions are required to mitigate the change
Follow-up on change management with change review meetings/ conference calls

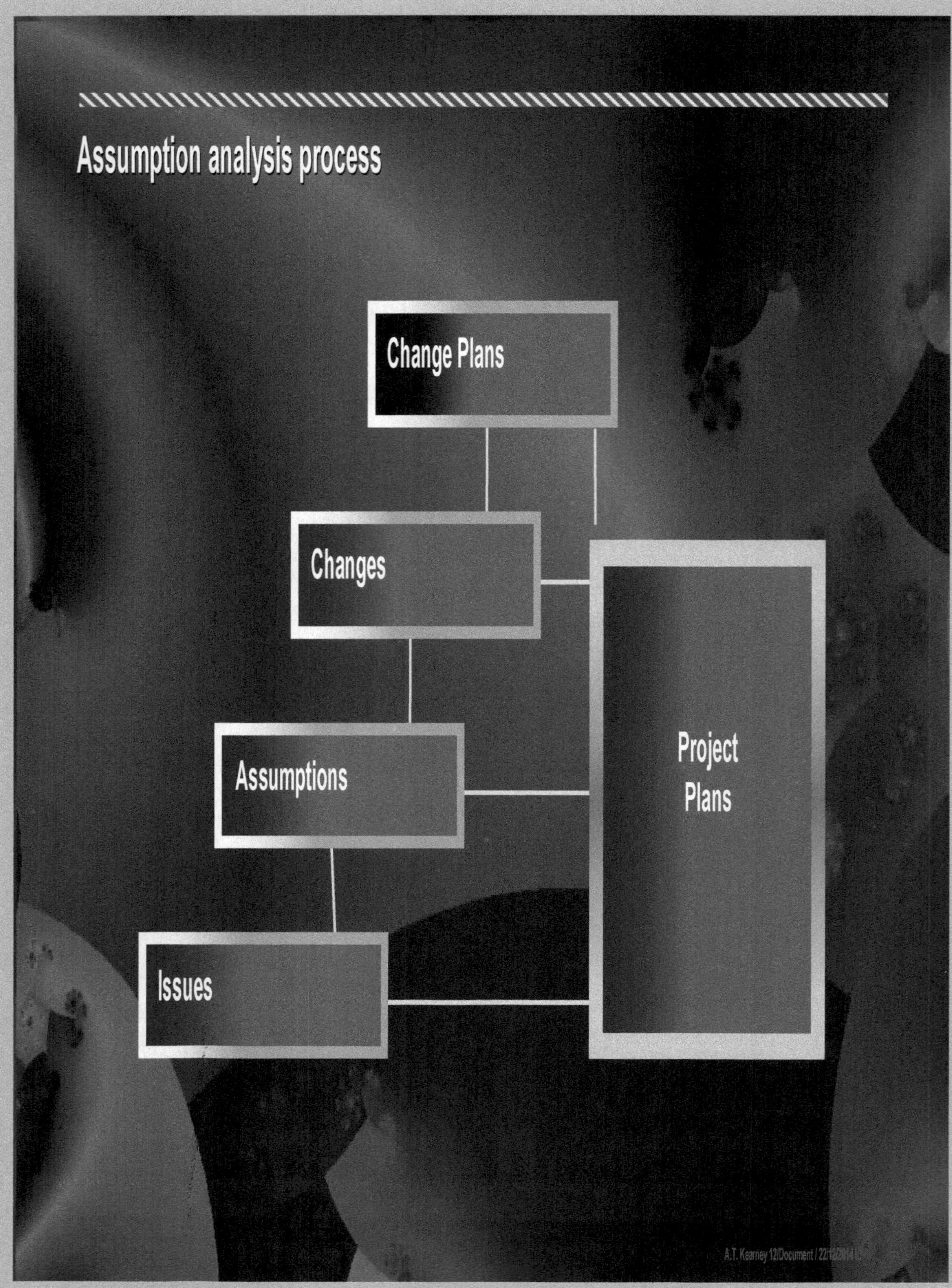
Assumption analysis process
Change Plans
Changes
Assumptions
Issues
Project
Plans

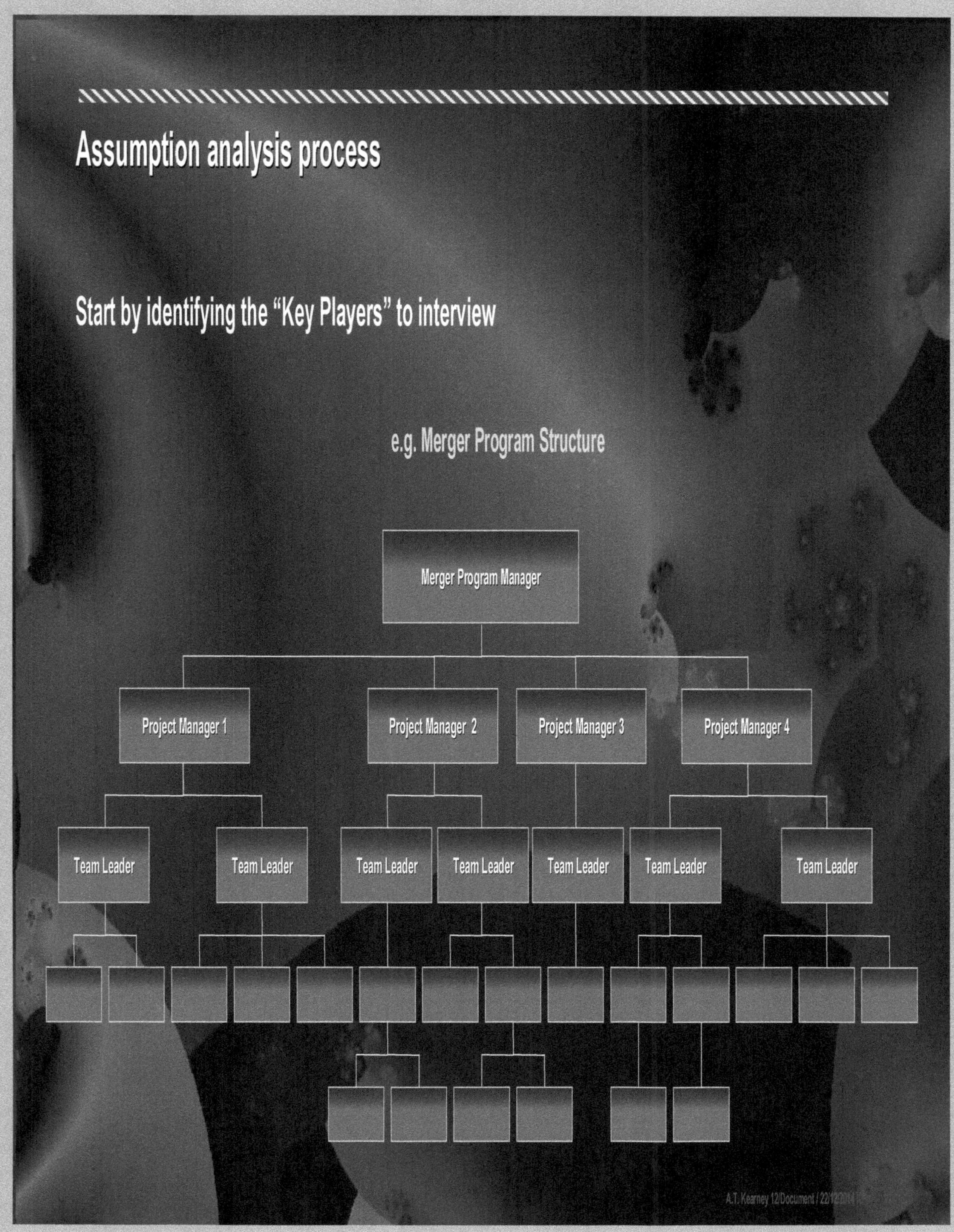
Assumption analysis process
Start by identifying the "Key Players" to interview
e.g. Merger Program Structure
Merger Program Manager
Project Manager 1
Project Manager 2
Project Manager 3
Project Manager 4
Team Leader
Team Leader
Team Leader
Team Leader
Team Leader
Team Leader
Team Leader
A.T. Kearney 12/Document

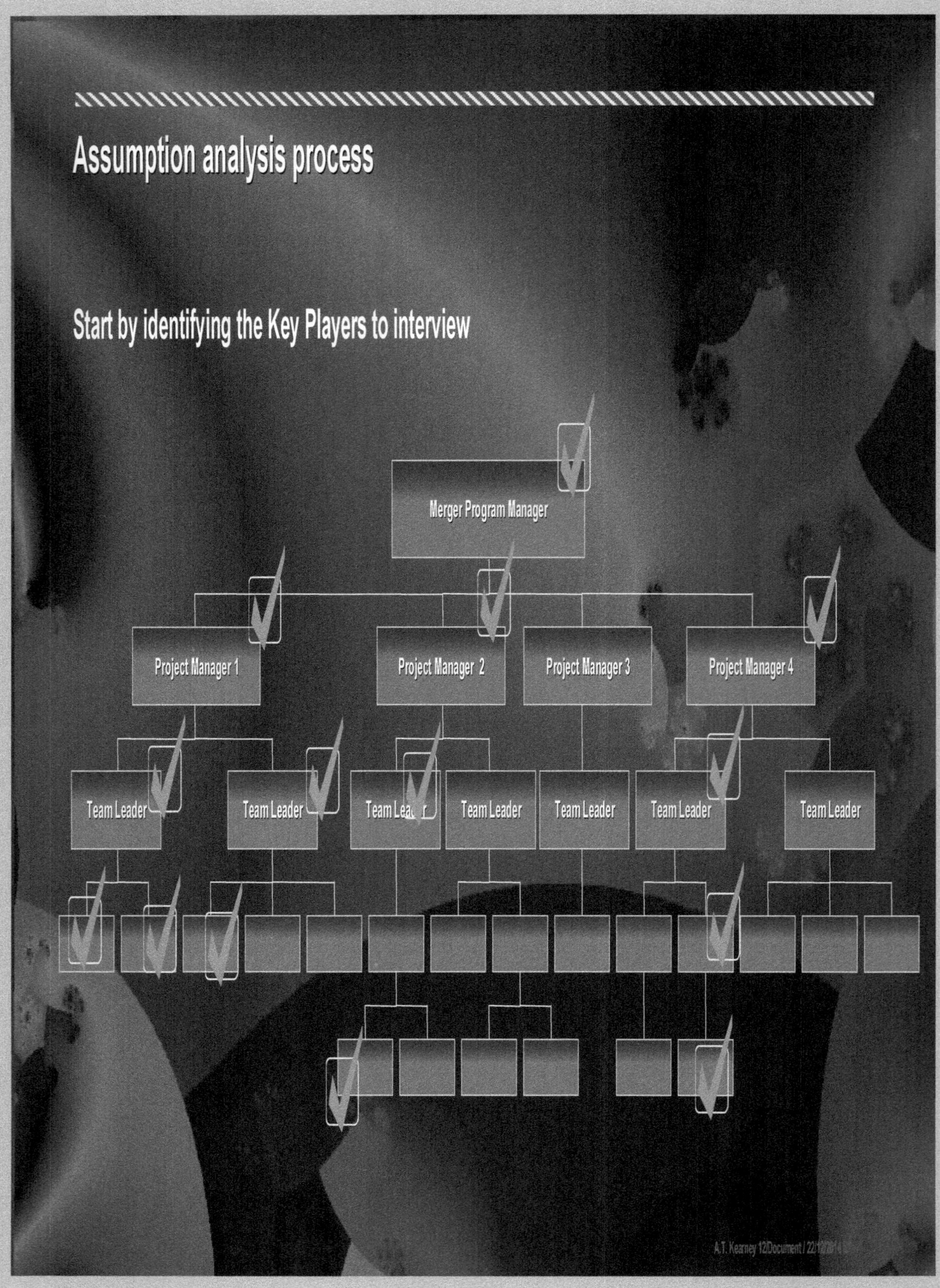
Assumption analysis process
Start by identifying the Key Players to interview
Merger Program Manager
Project Manager 1
Project Manager 2
Project Manager 3
Project Manager 4
Team Leader
Team Leader
Team Leader
Team Leader
Team Leader
Team Leader
Team Leader

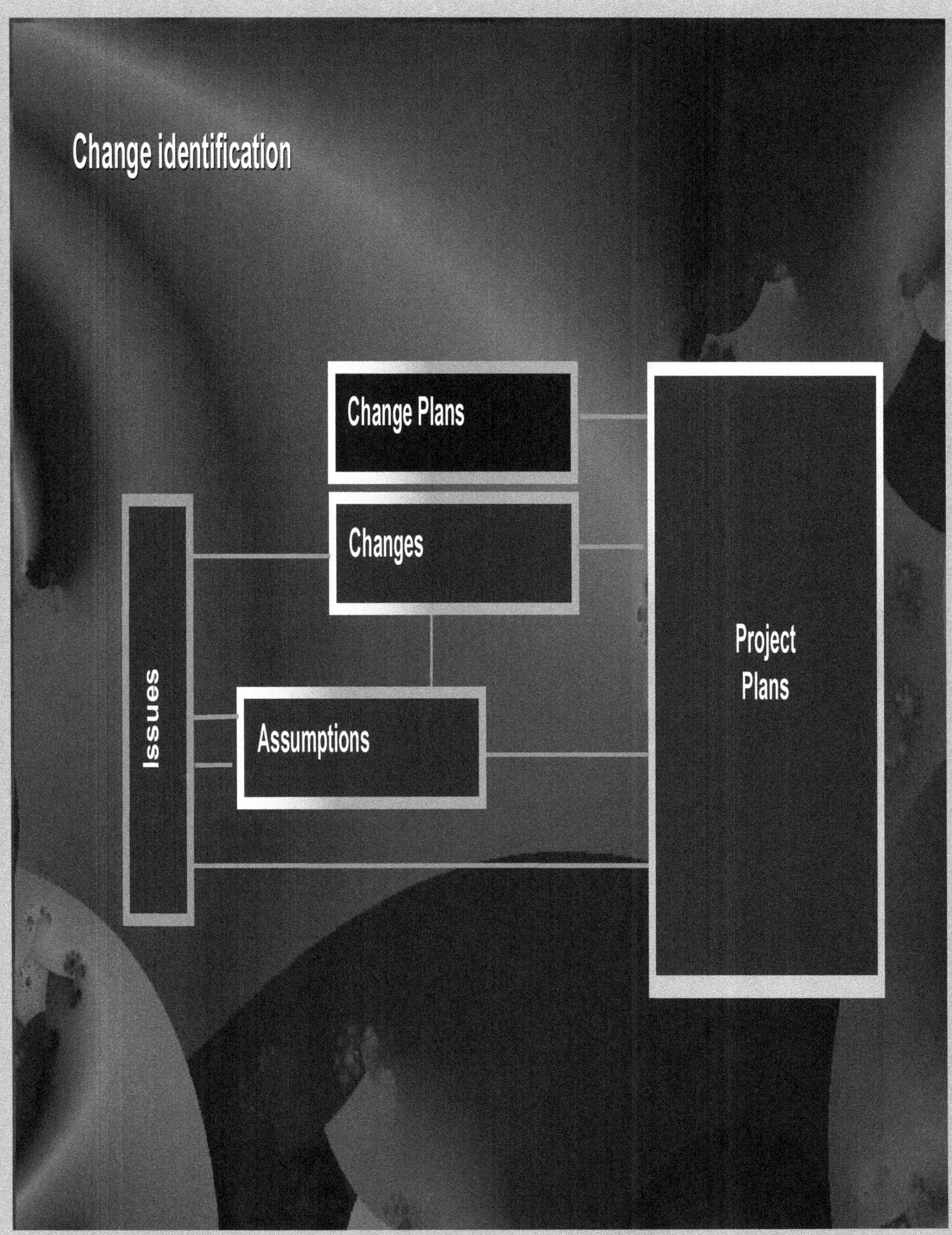
Change identification
Change Plans
Changes
Issues
Assumptions
Project
Plans

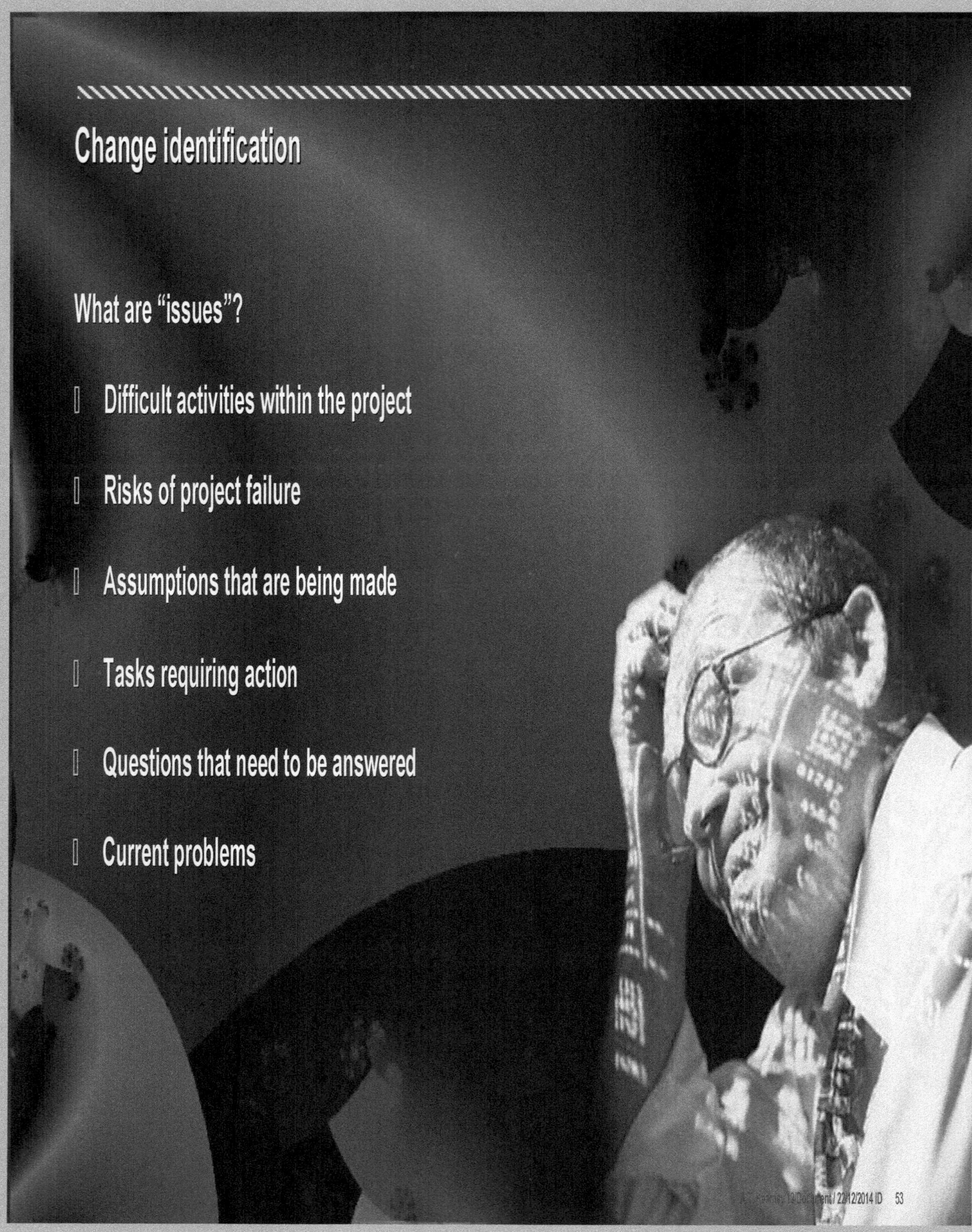
Change identification
What are "issues"?
Difficult activities within the project
Risks of project failure
Assumptions that are being made
Tasks requiring action
Questions that need to be answered
Current problems
53

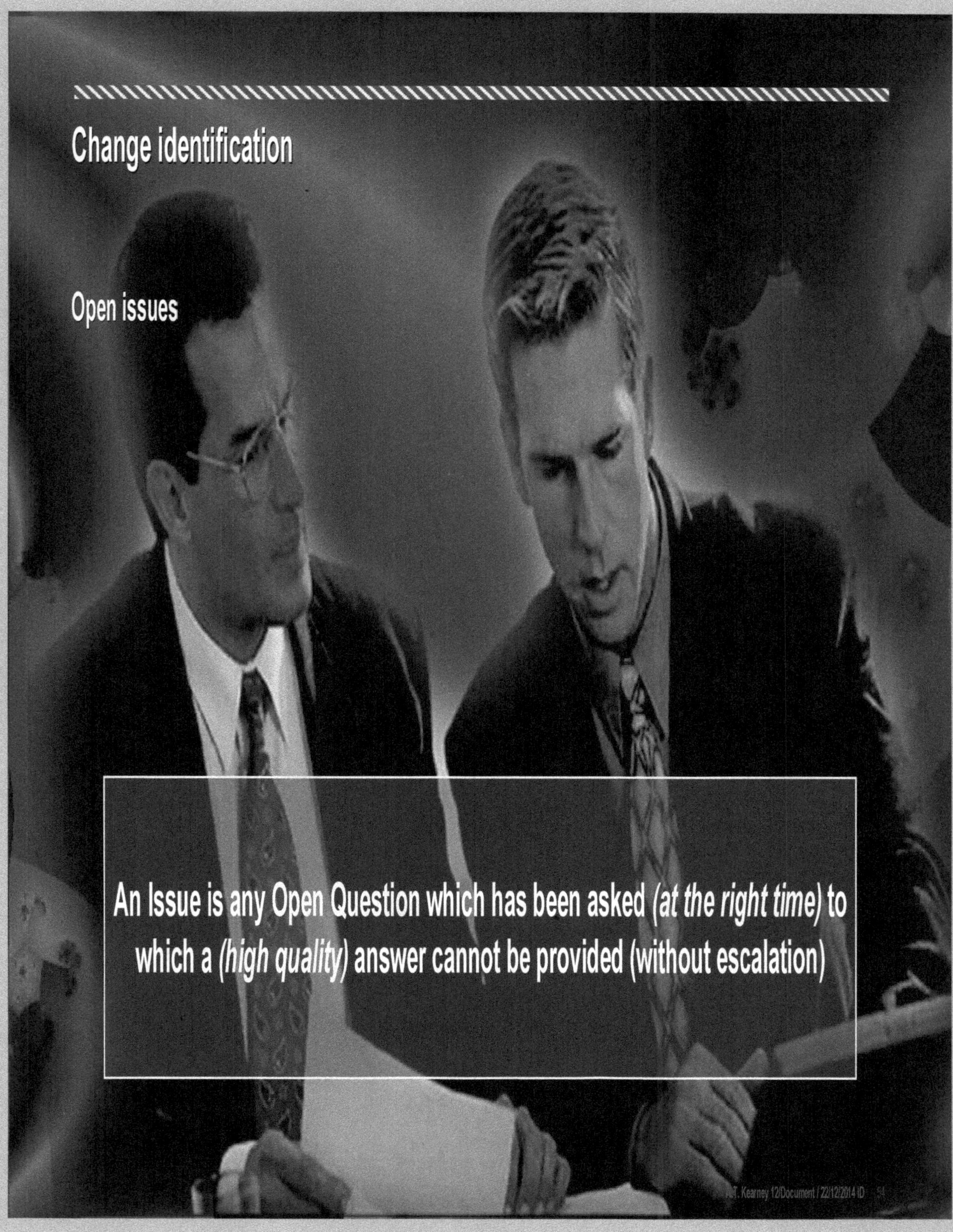
Change identification
Open issues
An Issue is any Open Question which has been asked (at the right time) to which a (high quality) answer cannot be provided (without escalation)

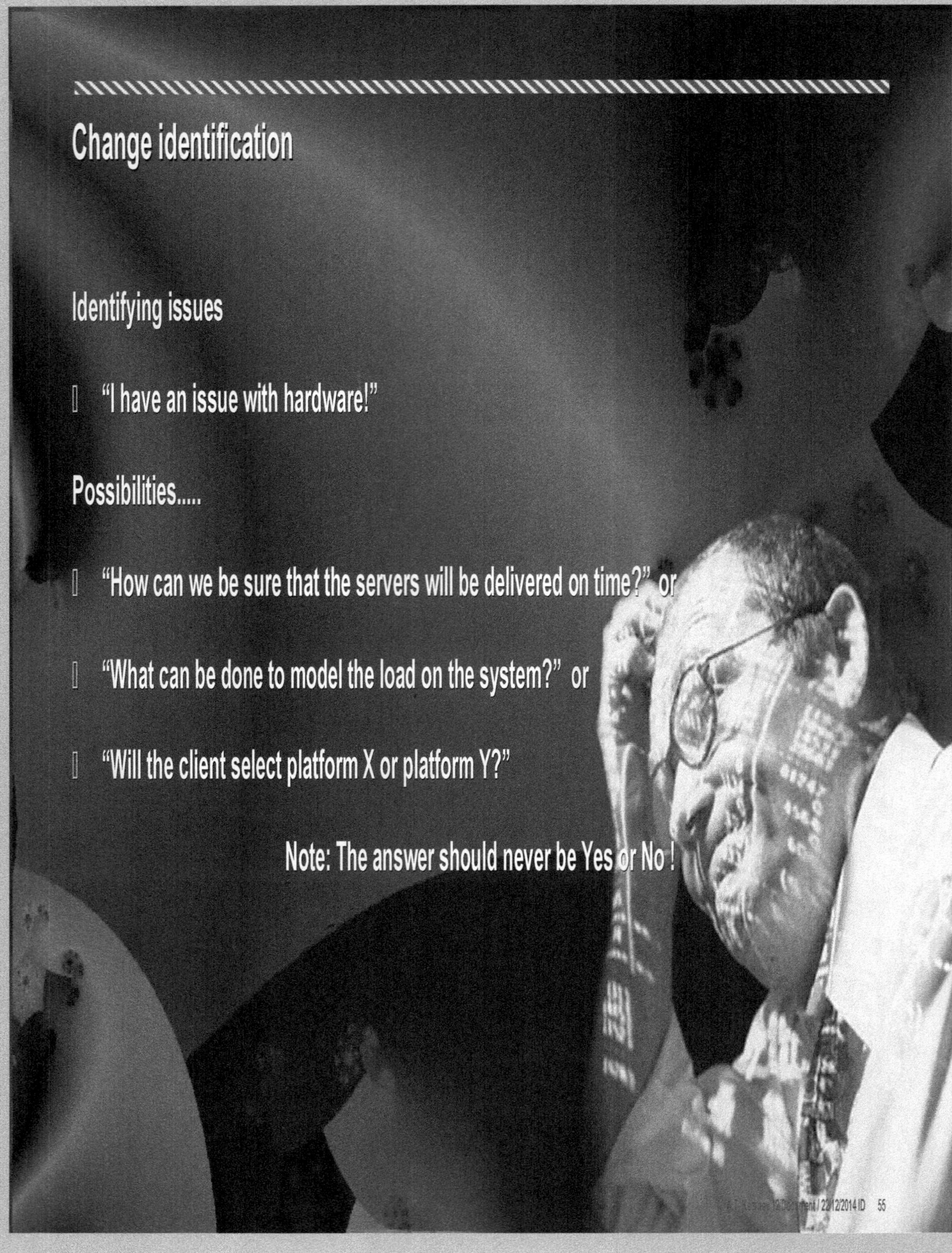
Change identification
Identifying issues
"I have an issue with hardware!"
Possibilities.....
"How can we be sure that the servers will be delivered on time?" or
"What can be done to model the load on the system?" or
"Will the client select platform X or platform Y?"
Note: The answer should never be Yes or No !
55

Change identification
Prioritising Issues
Issue size – How big is the issue (A, B, C, D)
A
B
C
D

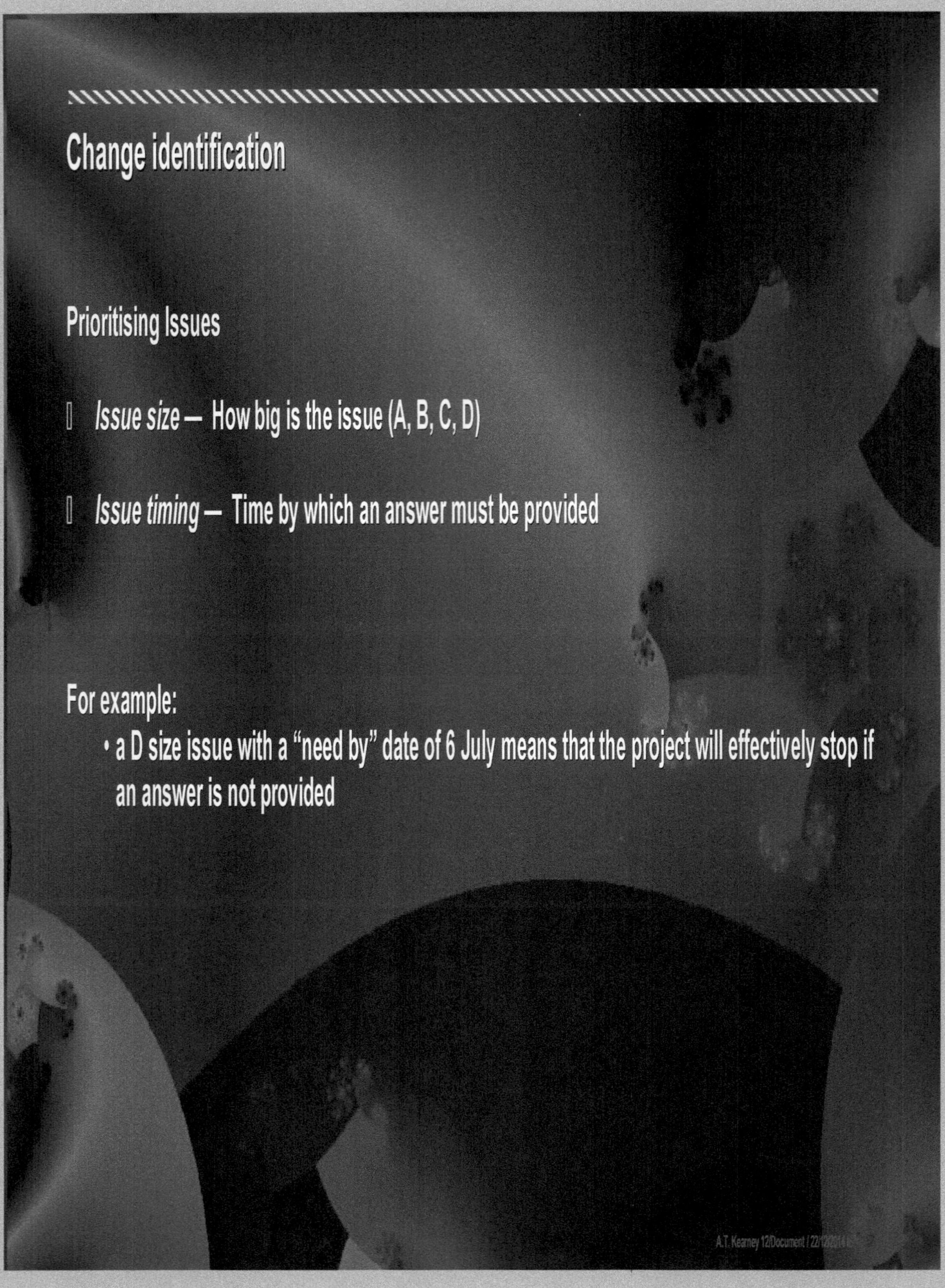
Change identification
Prioritising Issues
Issue size – How big is the issue (A, B, C, D)
Issue timing – Time by which an answer must be provided
For example:
• a D size issue with a "need by" date of 6 July means that the project will effectively stop if an answer is not provided

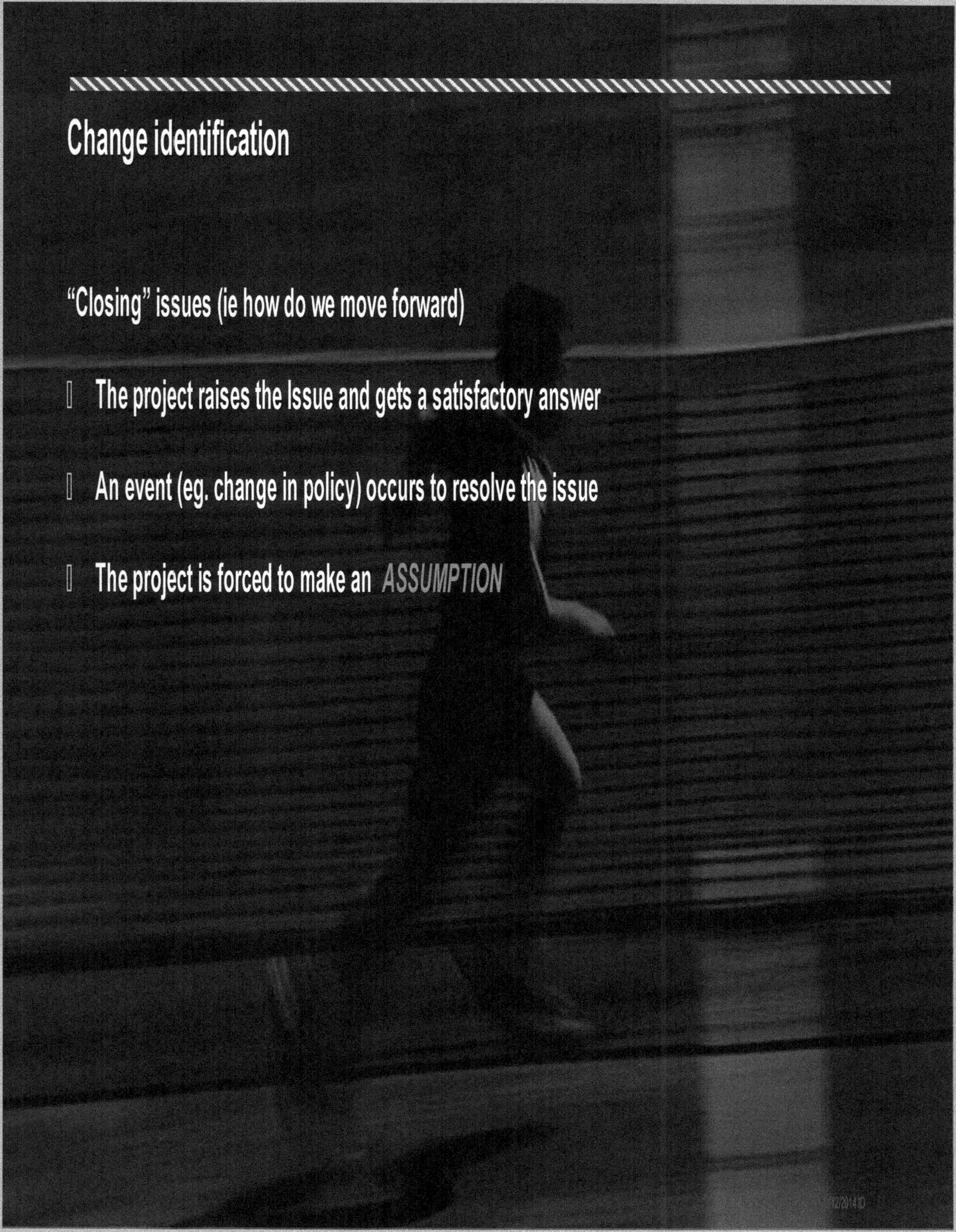

Change identification

"Closing" issues (ie how do we move forward)

- The project raises the Issue and gets a satisfactory answer
- An event (eg. change in policy) occurs to resolve the issue
- The project is forced to make an *ASSUMPTION*

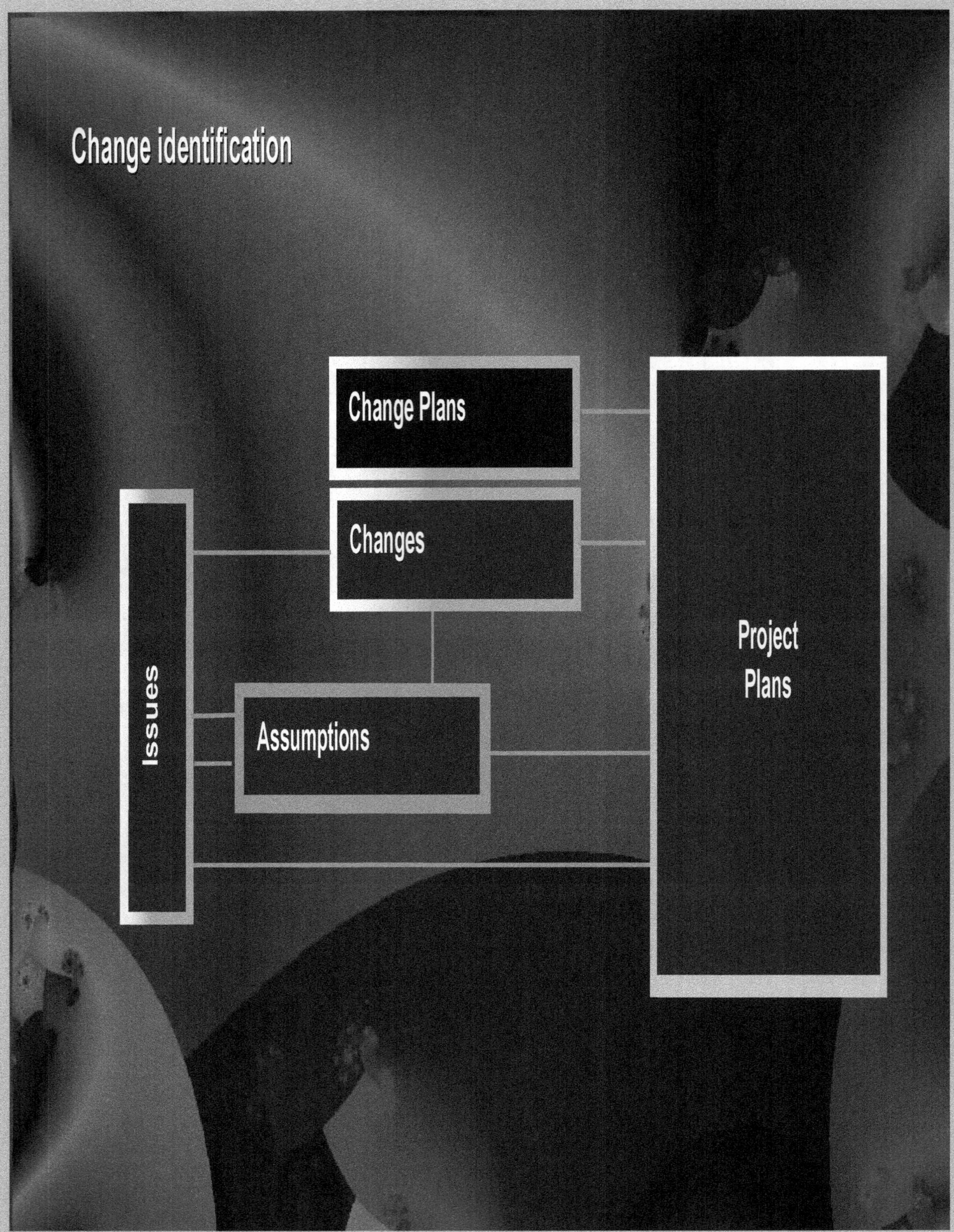
Change identification
Change Plans
Changes
Issues
Assumptions
Project
Plans

Change identification
Looking for Issues or Assumptions?
Note: You should only capture significant Issues when the plans have not been established or the plans are very unstable
Otherwise – Focus on assumptions
Rule of thumb: Start of a project = Issues;
Project plans = Assumptions
A.T. Kearney 12/Document / 22/12/2014

Assumption analysis

There are only three fundamental reasons why a project or programme fails

- The assumptions we make go wrong

about.....
  - Dependencies
  - Milestones
  - Resources
  - Complexity etc.

- We fail to understand the significance of the assumptions we make
  - We underestimate the importance of the assumptions
  - We overestimate the importance of the assumptions

- We fail to communicate the assumptions we make

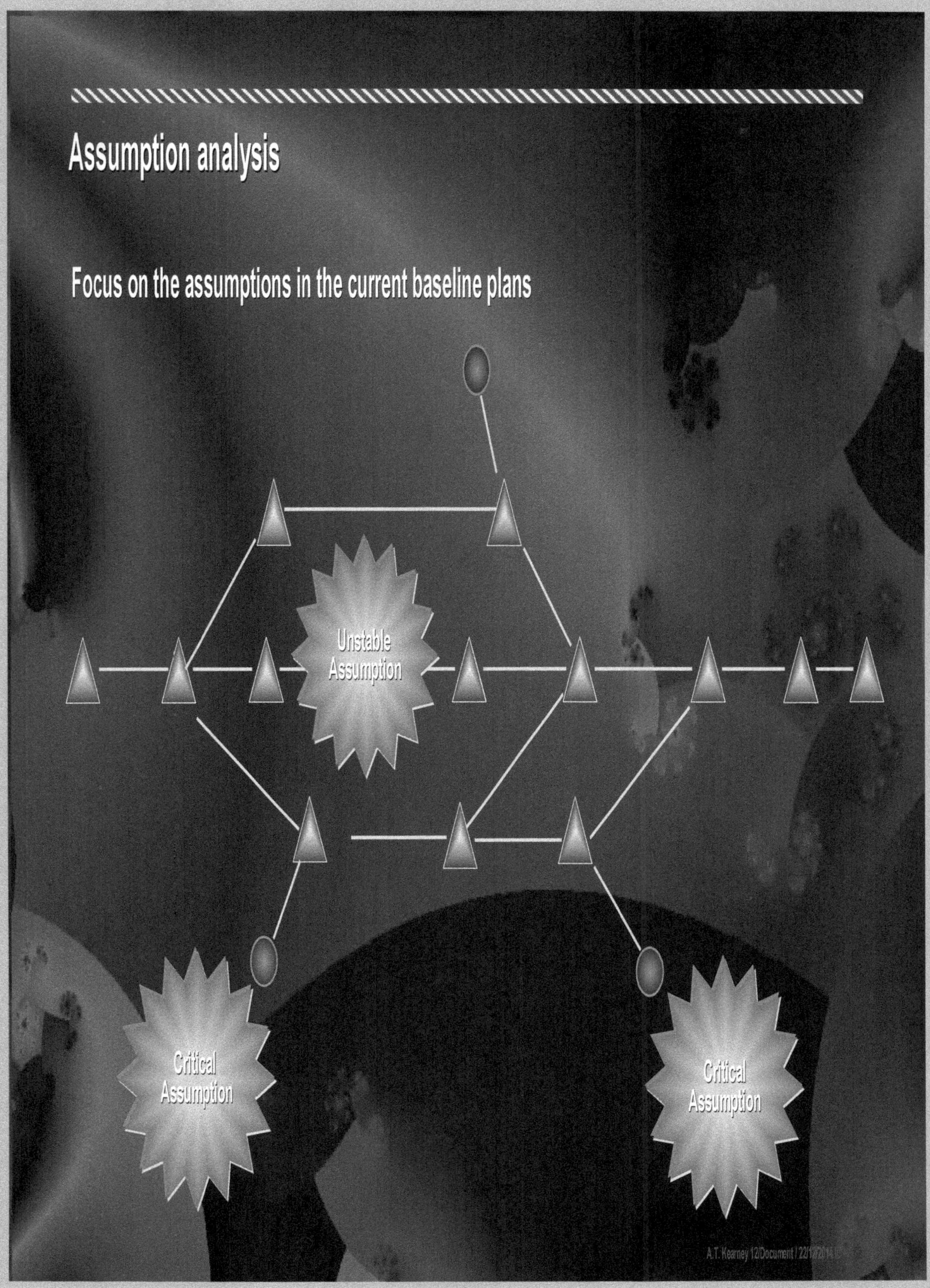
Assumption analysis
Focus on the assumptions in the current baseline plans
Unstable Assumption
Critical Assumption
Critical Assumption

Assumption analysis

What is an assumption?

- Definition: An Assumption is a single, simple, positive or negative statement

  ie "will" or "will not"

("What needs to happen for your plans to deliver?")

eg "The contract will be let to a single supplier"

or "Users will be available to support UAT"

or "It will not be necessary to get business sign-off for minor change requests"

A.T. Kearney 12/Document / 22/12/20[illegible]

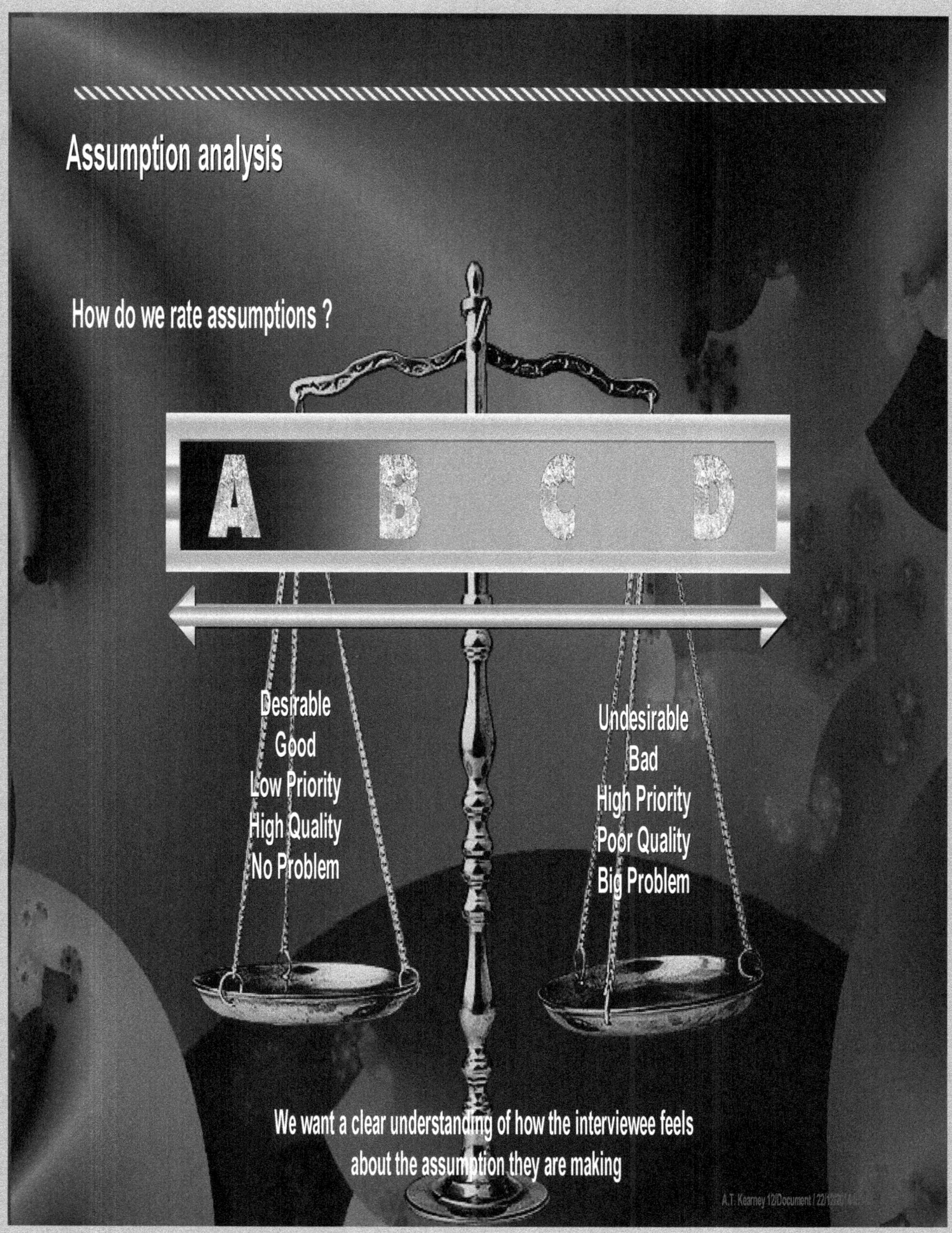
Assumption analysis
How do we rate assumptions ?
A
B
C
D
Desirable
Good
Low Priority
High Quality
No Problem
Undesirable
Bad
High Priority
Poor Quality
Big Problem
We want a clear understanding of how the interviewee feels
about the assumption they are making

Assumption analysis
Assumptions have two distinct dimensions
A B C D
Need to rate both the
Stability and Sensitivity of each assumption
A.T. Kearney 12/Document

Assumption analysis

Two Key Characteristics of any Assumption:

- Stability: How stable is the Assumption ? i.e. how confident are we?
  A = very stable/confident
  D = very unstable/unconfident

- Sensitivity: How sensitive is the project to the Assumptions i.e. how much does it matter if the assumption is incorrect?
  A = not sensitive/minimal impact
  D = very sensitive/critical impact

In general: A = No problem, D = Big problem

A.T. Kearney 12/Document /

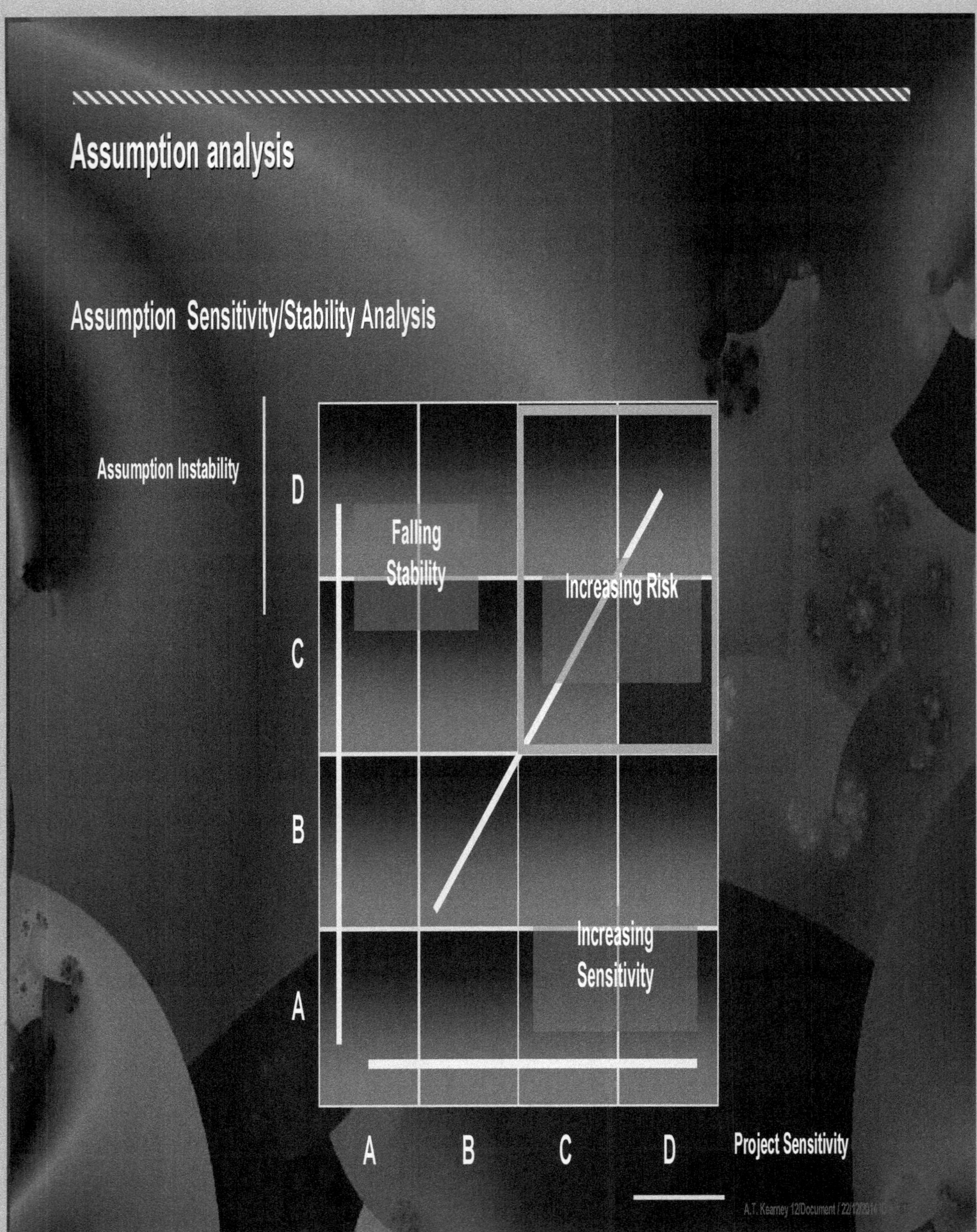
Assumption analysis
Assumption Sensitivity/Stability Analysis
Assumption Instability
D
C
B
A
Falling Stability
Increasing Risk
Increasing Sensitivity
A
B
C
D
Project Sensitivity
A.T. Kearney 12/Document /

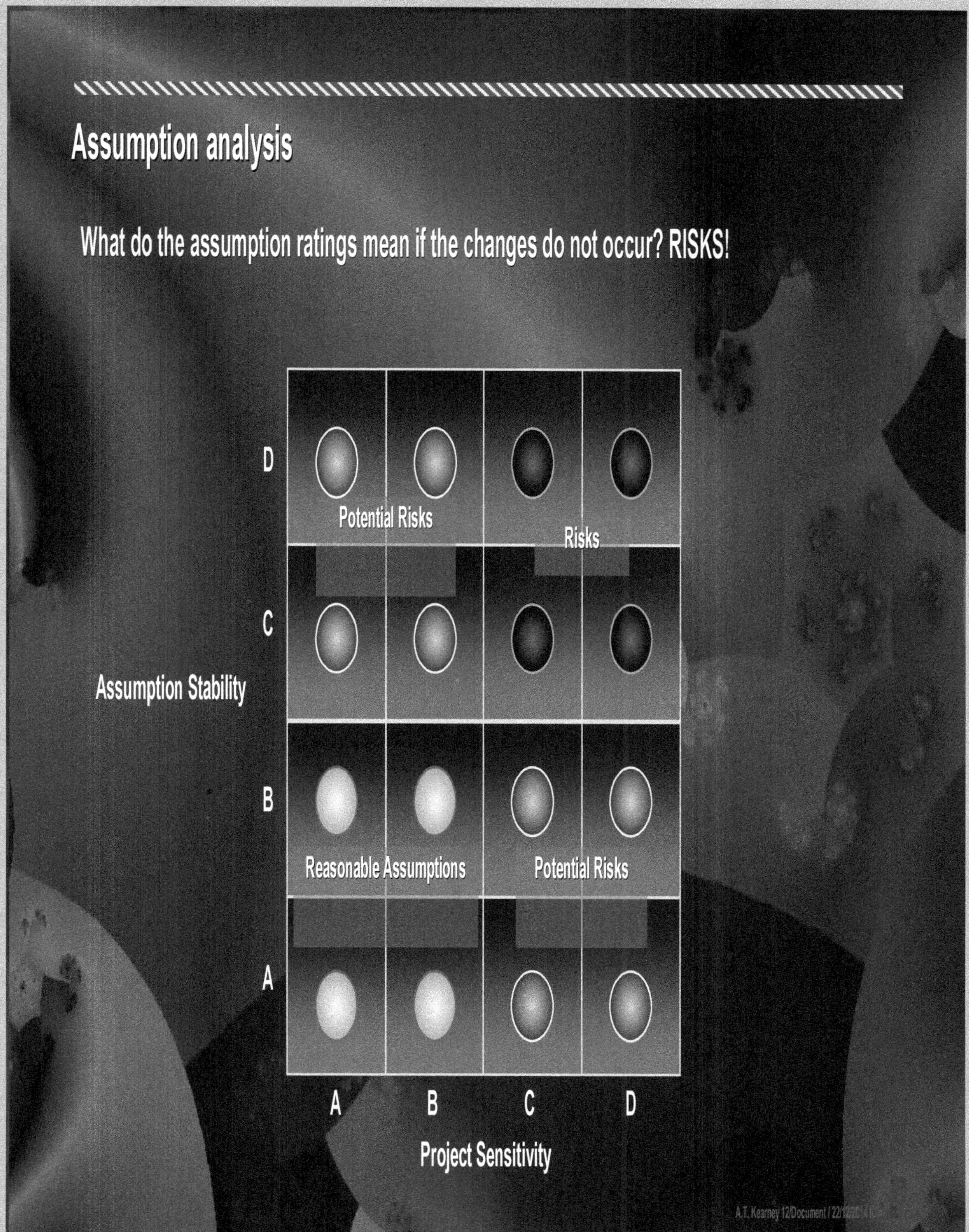
Assumption analysis
What do the assumption ratings mean if the changes do not occur? RISKS!
D
C
B
A
Potential Risks
Risks
Assumption Stability
Reasonable Assumptions
Potential Risks
A
B
C
D
Project Sensitivity

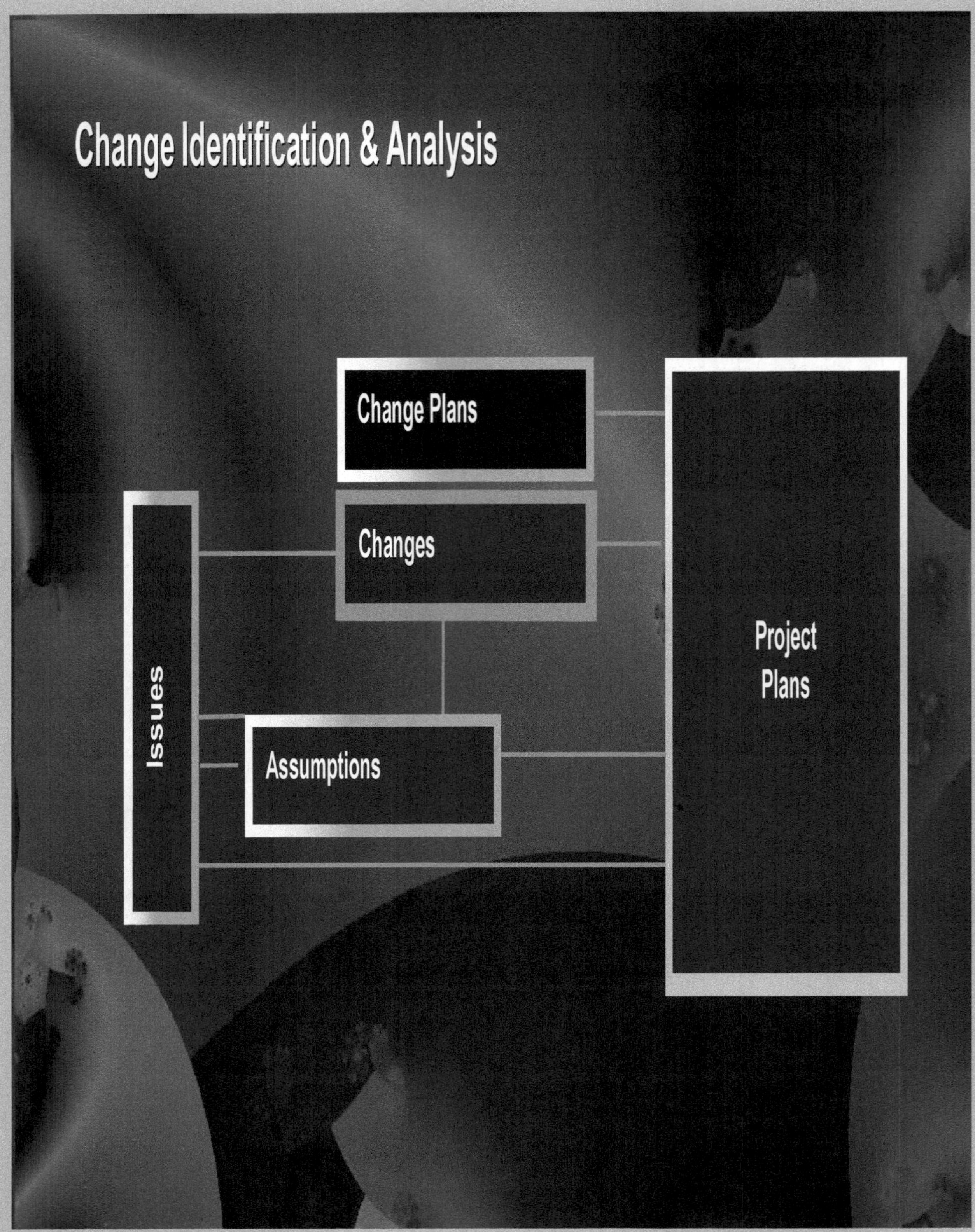
Change Identification & Analysis
Change Plans
Changes
Issues
Assumptions
Project Plans

Changes

Expressing Changes clearly

- Definition: A Change is a simple statement of the form:

"IF"	*Assumption proves incorrect*
"THEN"	*Describe the impact*

- An easier way is: *Assumption statement*

  If not/then *Describe the impact*

A.T. Kearney 12/Document / 22/12/2014

Assumption analysis process

Example

- *Issue*: "When will System X be delivered so that interface testing can commence?" (Rated Size = C, Timing = 1 July)
- *Assumption*: "System X will be available by 1 August so that interface testing can commence" (Sens = D, Stab = C)
- *Risk if no change occurs*: "IF System X is not available by 1 August THEN the interface testing cannot begin leading to delays to the implementation date"

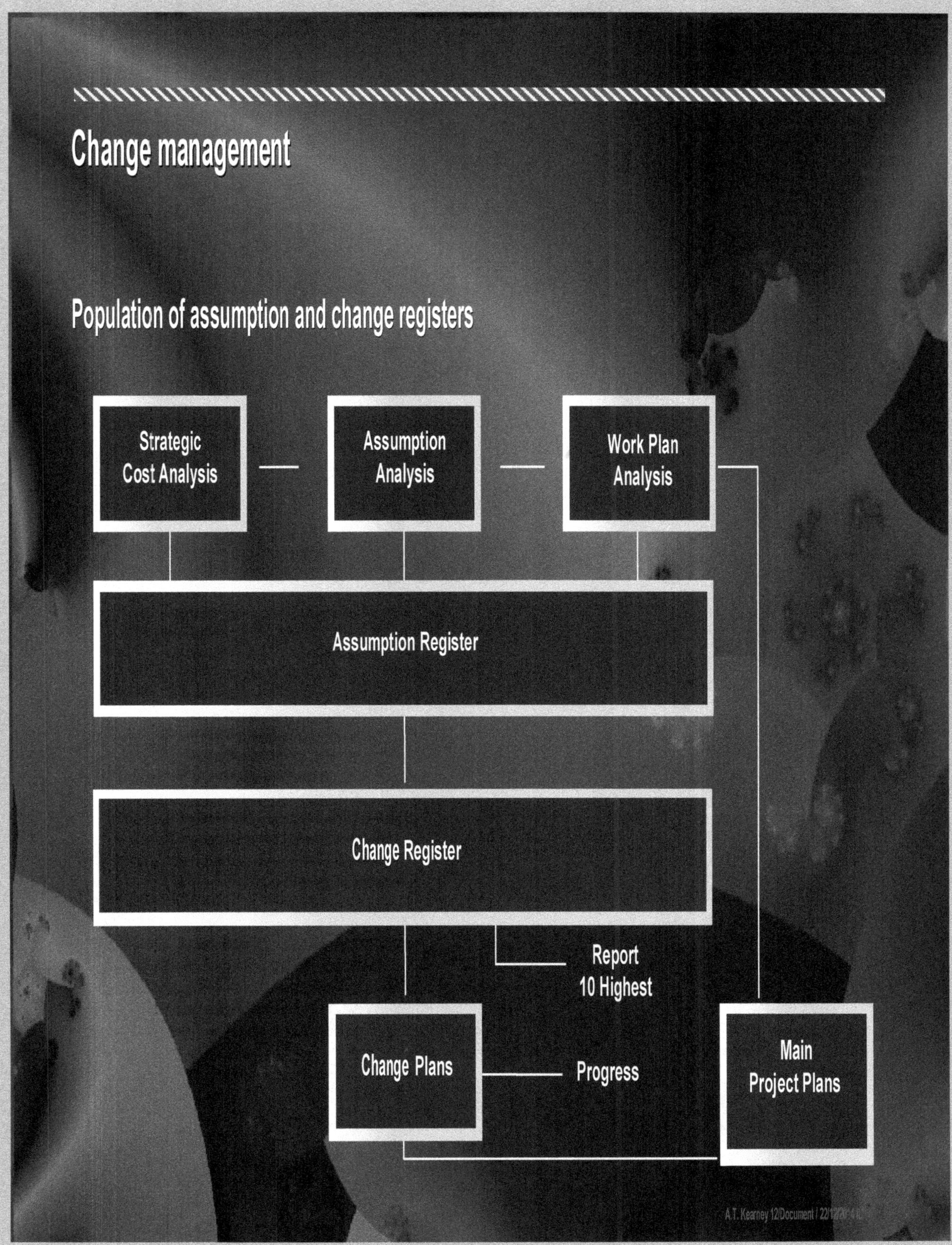
Change management
Population of assumption and change registers
Strategic Cost Analysis
Assumption Analysis
Work Plan Analysis
Assumption Register
Change Register
Report 10 Highest
Change Plans
Progress
Main Project Plans

Change prioritisation
Why prioritise?
Focus onto critical Changes
Attack risks if no changes at the right time
Direct project resources
A.T. Kearney 12/Document /

Change prioritisation

Classify Changes in terms of:

- Criticality – i.e. How would the Change impact the Critical Objectives of the project?
  Green = minor impact,
  Amber = significant impact,
  Red = critical impact
- Controllability – i.e. Is the Change likely to be managed/avoided? A = very likely, D = very unlikely
- Time – i.e. How urgent? - When will the Change start to impact the project ?

"When do we need to start taking action?"

A.T. Kearney 12/Document / 22/[illegible]

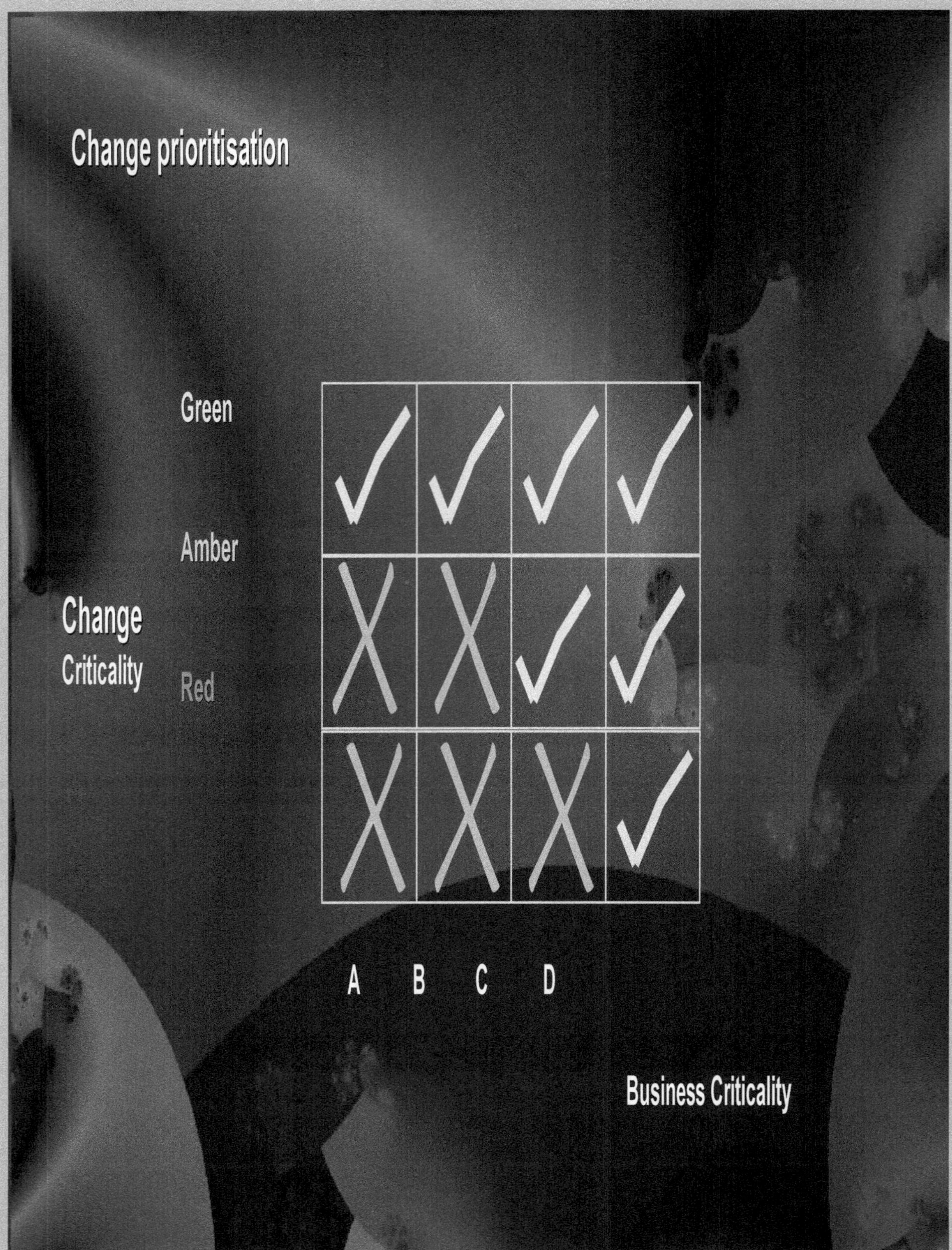
Change prioritisation
Green
Amber
Red
Change
Criticality
A
B
C
D
Business Criticality

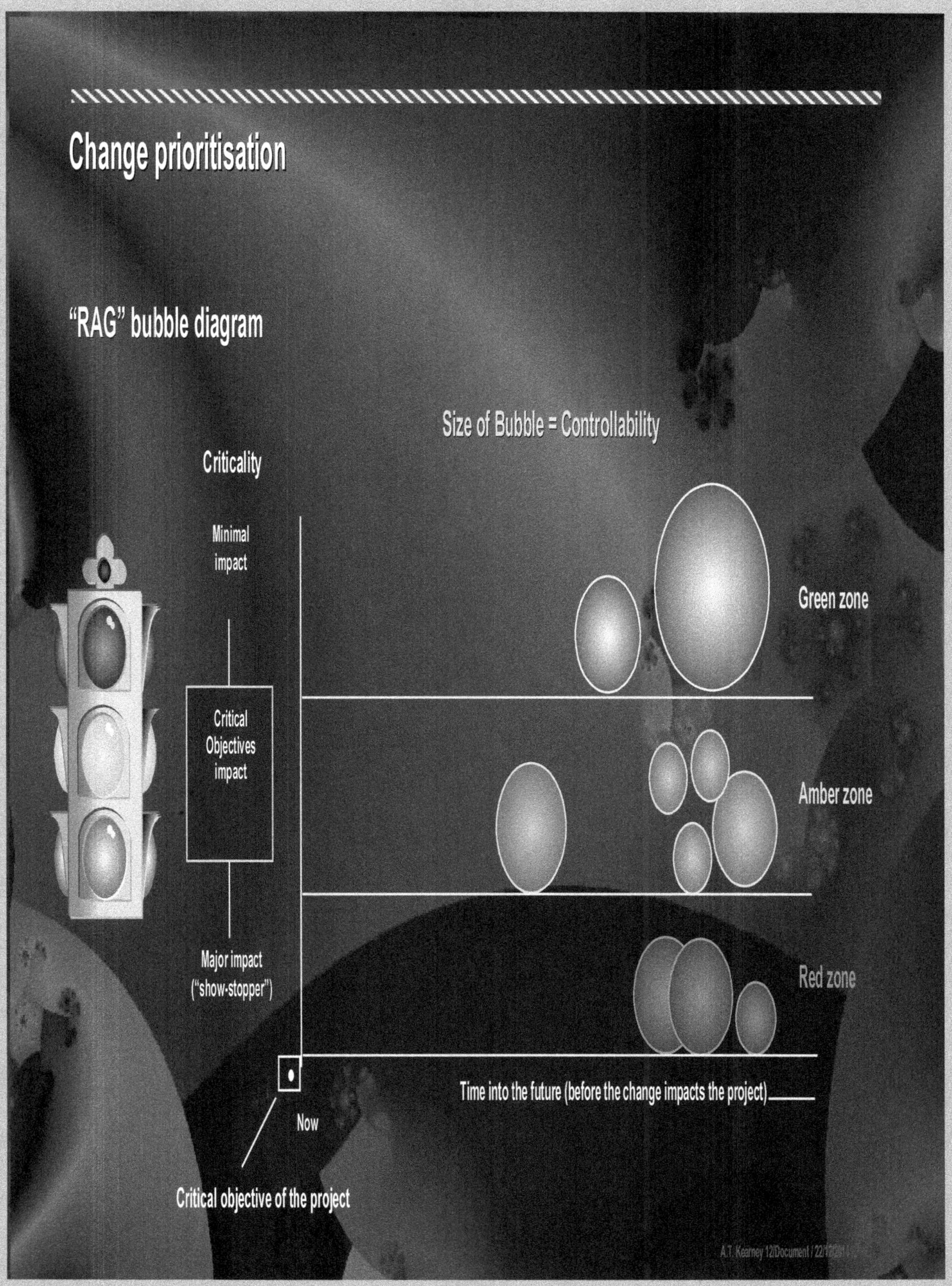
Change prioritisation
"RAG" bubble diagram
Size of Bubble = Controllability
Criticality
Minimal impact
Critical Objectives impact
Major impact ("show-stopper")
Green zone
Amber zone
Red zone
Now
Time into the future (before the change impacts the project)
Critical objective of the project

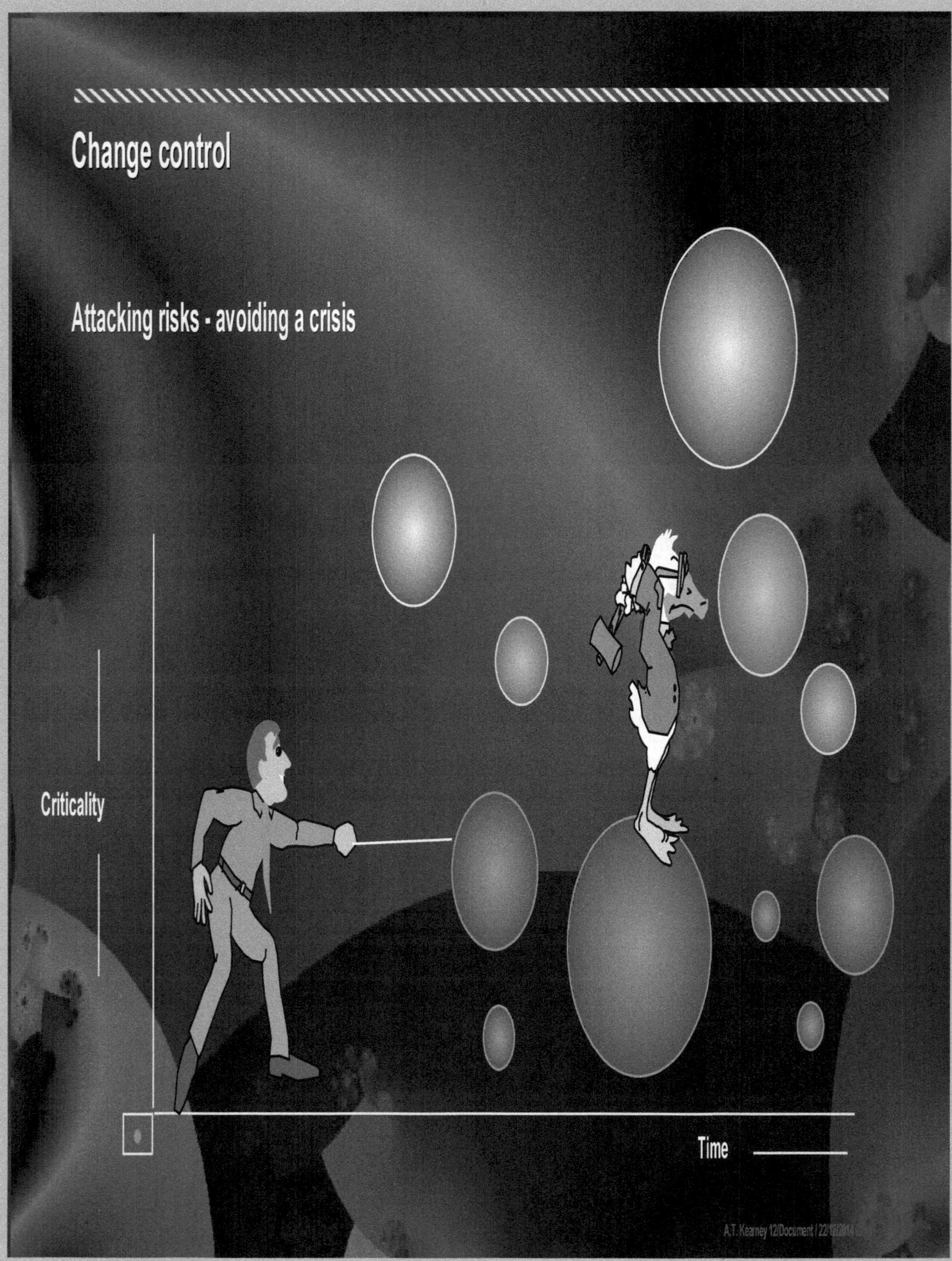
Change control
Attacking risks - avoiding a crisis
Criticality
Time

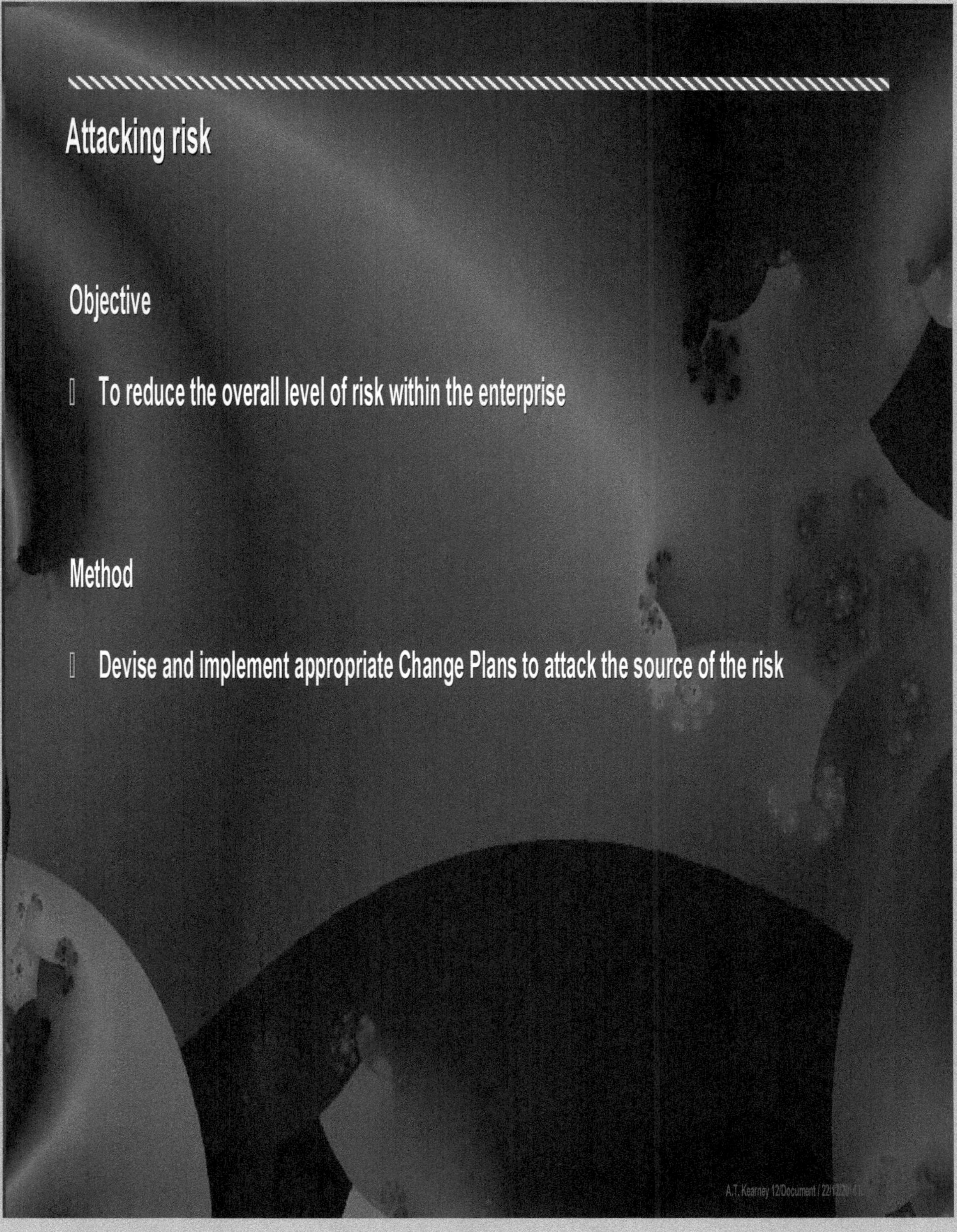
Attacking risk
Objective
To reduce the overall level of risk within the enterprise
Method
Devise and implement appropriate Change Plans to attack the source of the risk

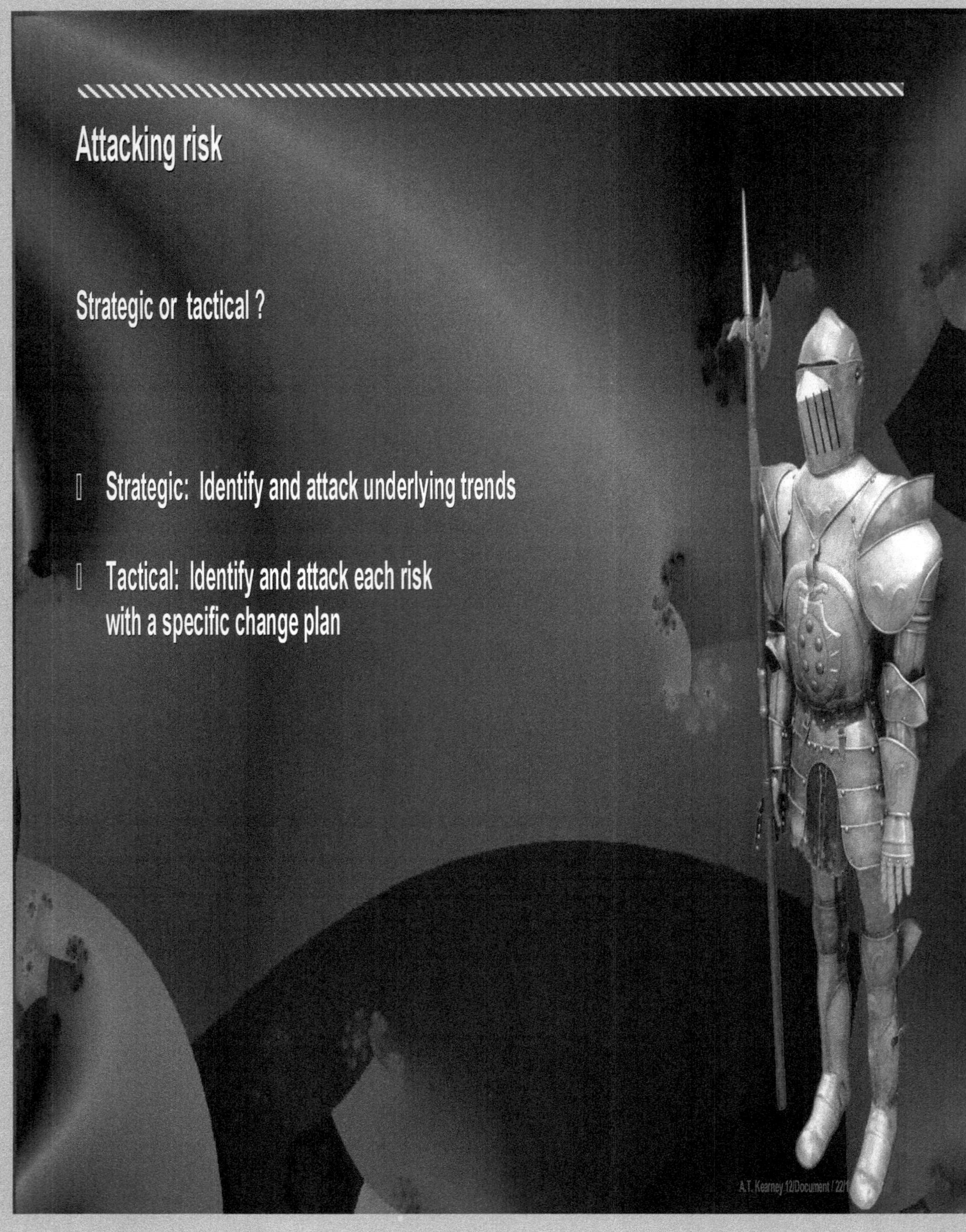
Attacking risk
Strategic or tactical ?
Strategic: Identify and attack underlying trends
Tactical: Identify and attack each risk
with a specific change plan
A.T. Kearney 12/Document / 22/

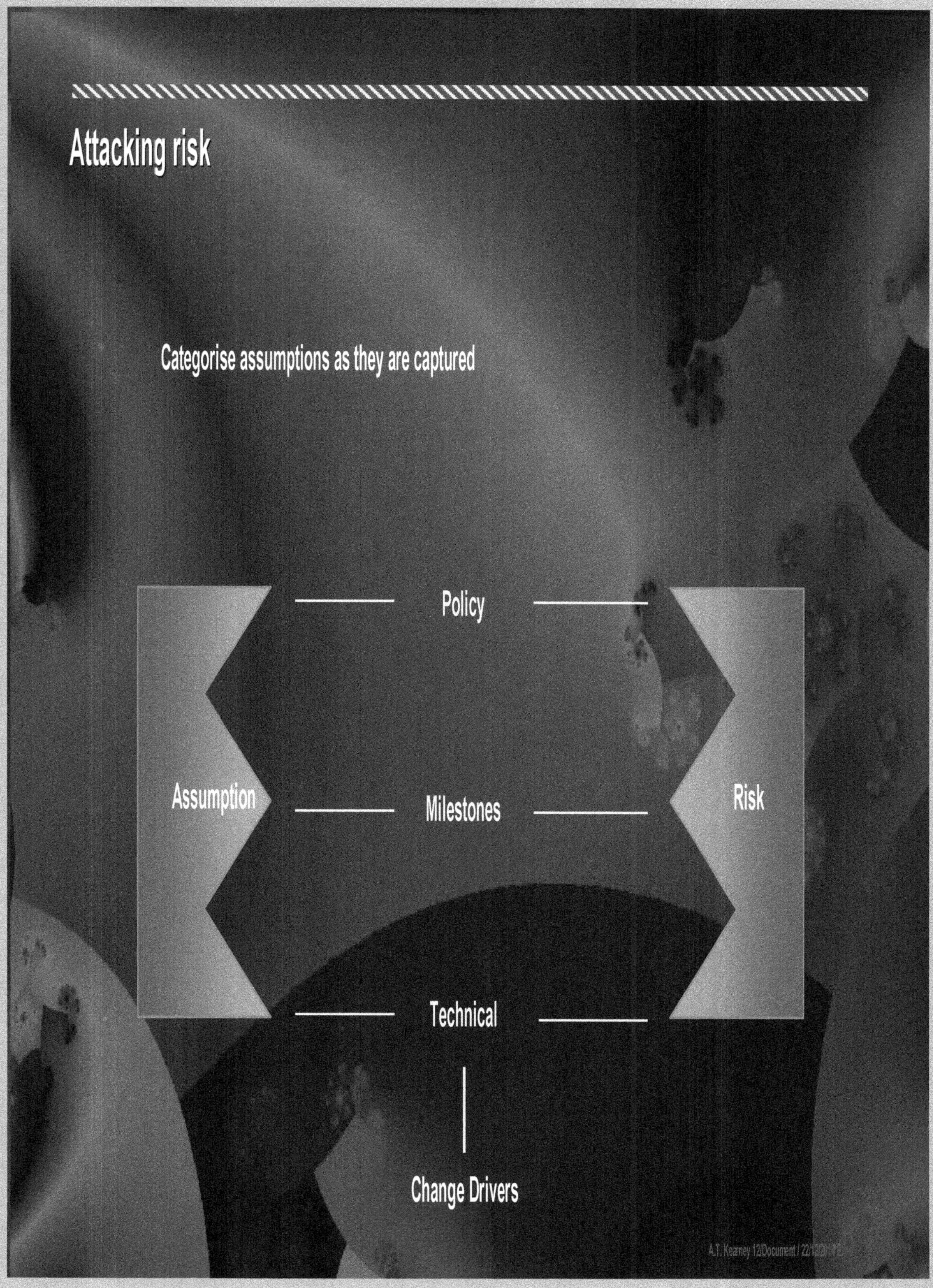
Attacking risk
Categorise assumptions as they are captured
Policy
Assumption
Milestones
Risk
Technical
Change Drivers

Attacking risk

Change driver chart – Example

Criticality

	Technical	*Milestone*	*Policy*	*Total*
Red	3	3	4	10
Amber	10	8	8	26
Green	5	7	8	20
Total	18	18	20	56

A.T. Kearney 12/Document /

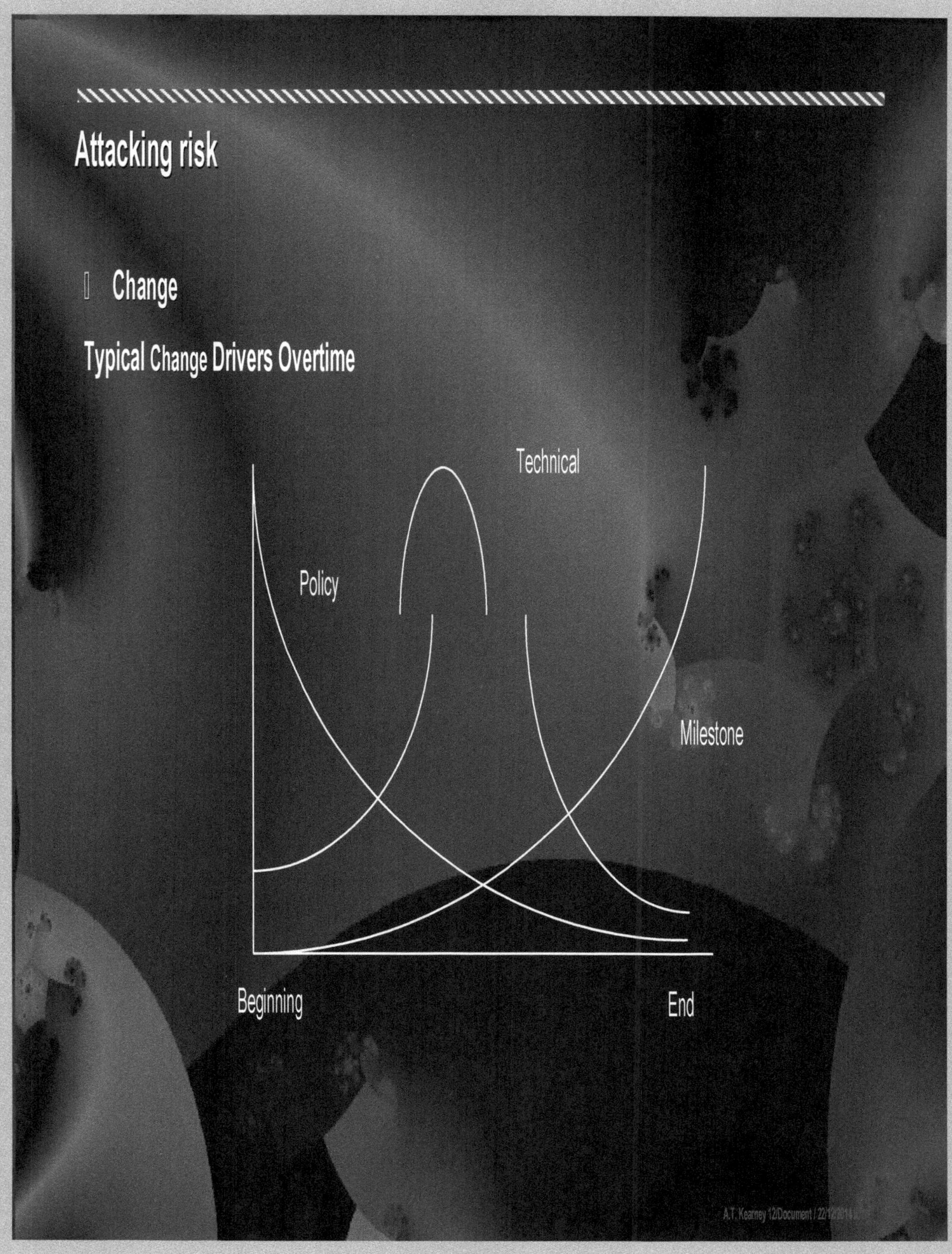
Attacking risk
Change
Typical Change Drivers Overtime
Technical
Policy
Milestone
Beginning
End
A.T. Kearney 12/Document

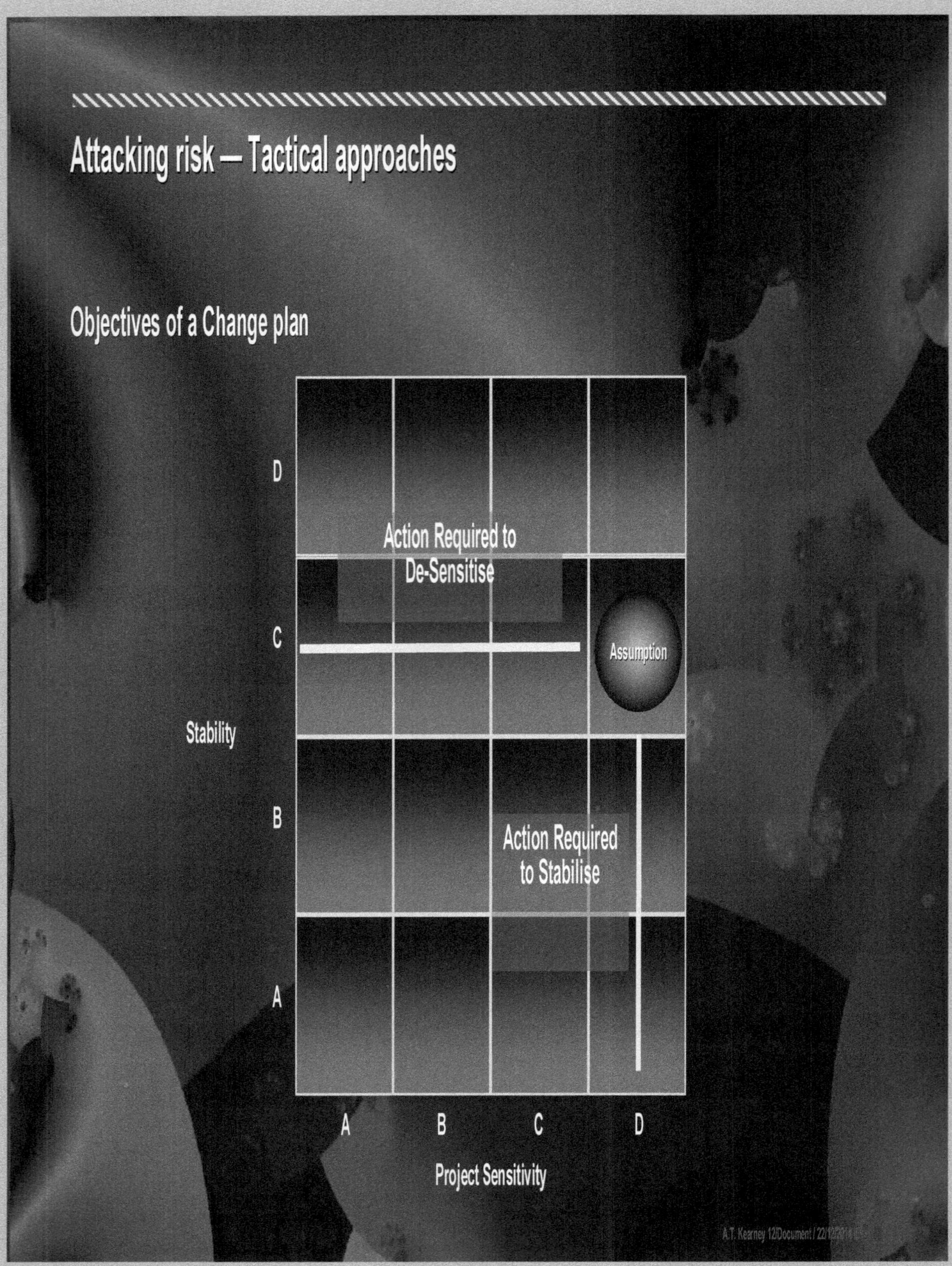
Attacking risk – Tactical approaches
Objectives of a Change plan
D
C
B
A
Stability
Action Required to
De-Sensitise
Assumption
Action Required
to Stabilise
A
B
C
D
Project Sensitivity
A.T. Kearney 12/Document / 22/12/2014

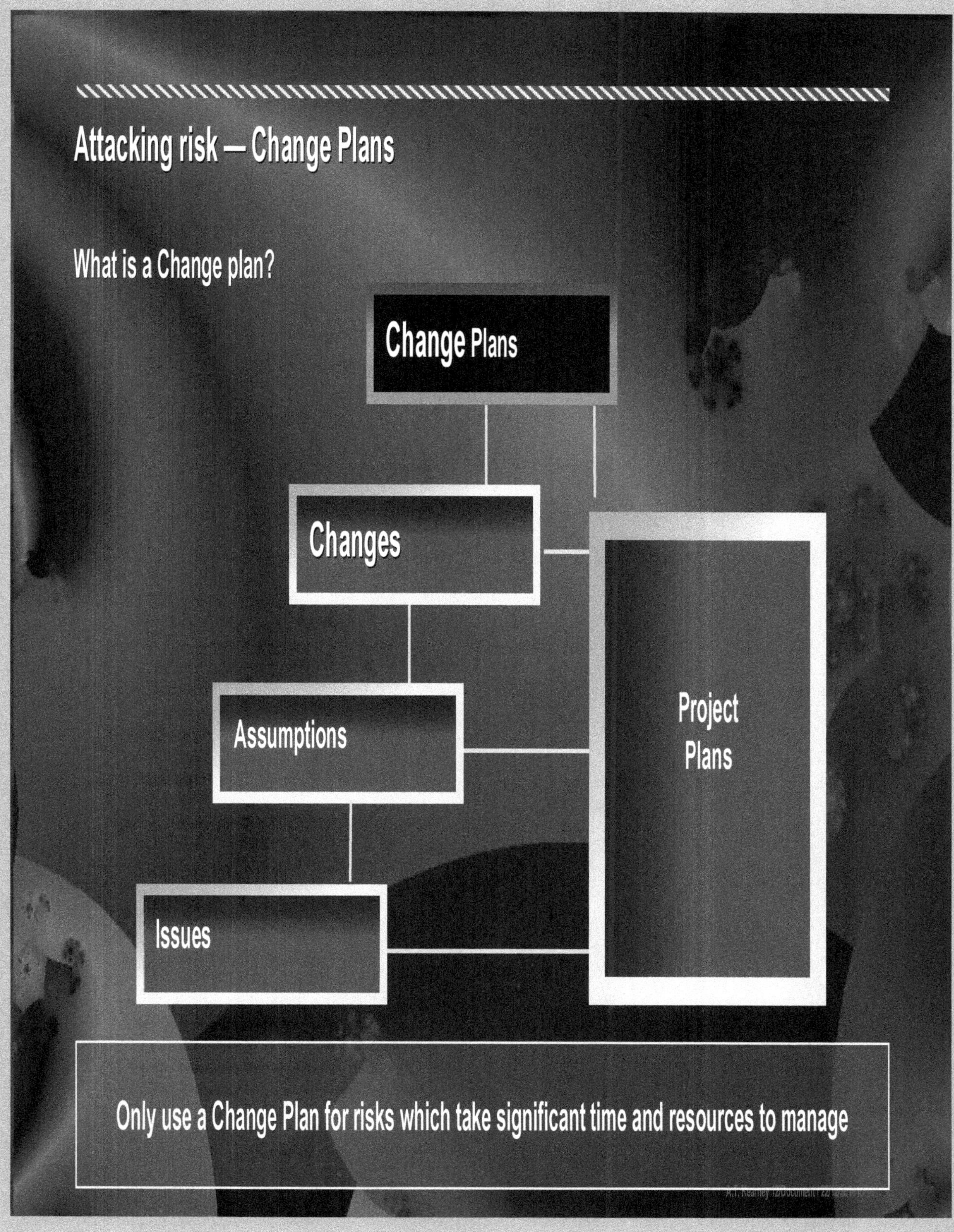
Attacking risk – Change Plans
What is a Change plan?
Change Plans
Changes
Assumptions
Issues
Project Plans
Only use a Change Plan for risks which take significant time and resources to manage

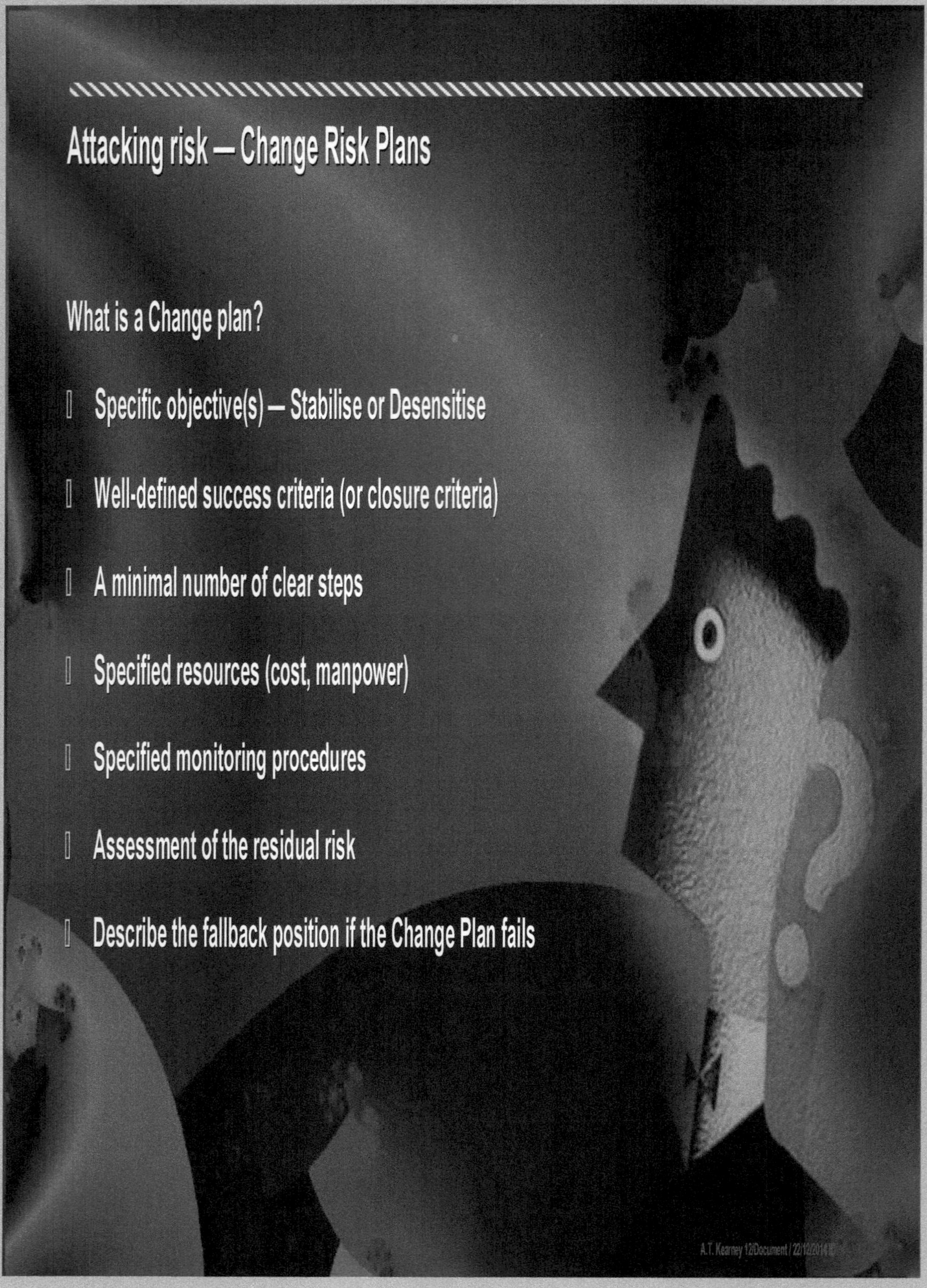
Attacking risk – Change Risk Plans
What is a Change plan?
Specific objective(s) – Stabilise or Desensitise
Well-defined success criteria (or closure criteria)
A minimal number of clear steps
Specified resources (cost, manpower)
Specified monitoring procedures
Assessment of the residual risk
Describe the fallback position if the Change Plan fails

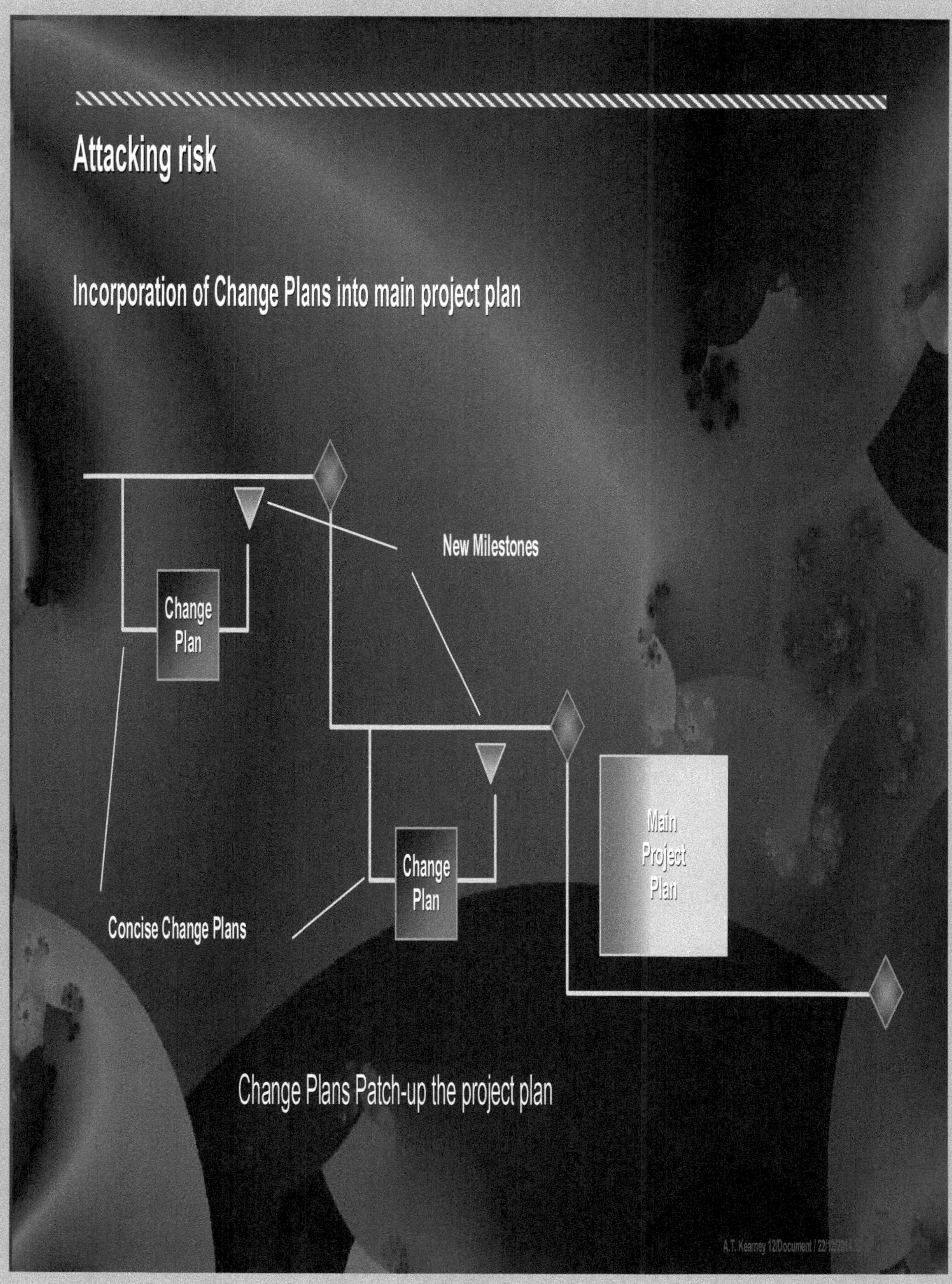
Attacking risk
Incorporation of Change Plans into main project plan
New Milestones
Change Plan
Change Plan
Main Project Plan
Concise Change Plans
Change Plans Patch-up the project plan

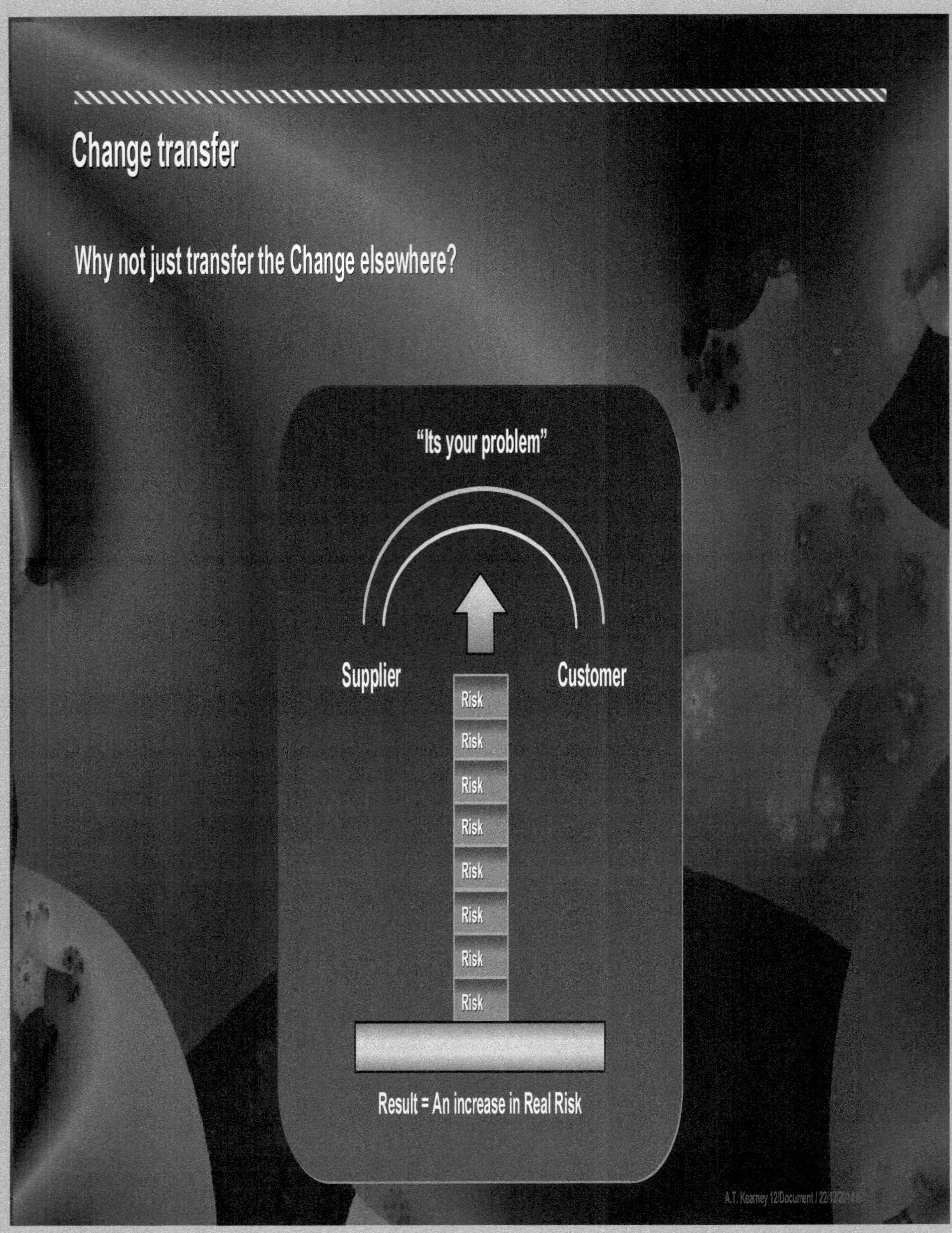
Change transfer
Why not just transfer the Change elsewhere?
"Its your problem"
Supplier
Customer
Risk
Risk
Risk
Risk
Risk
Risk
Risk
Risk
Result = An increase in Real Risk

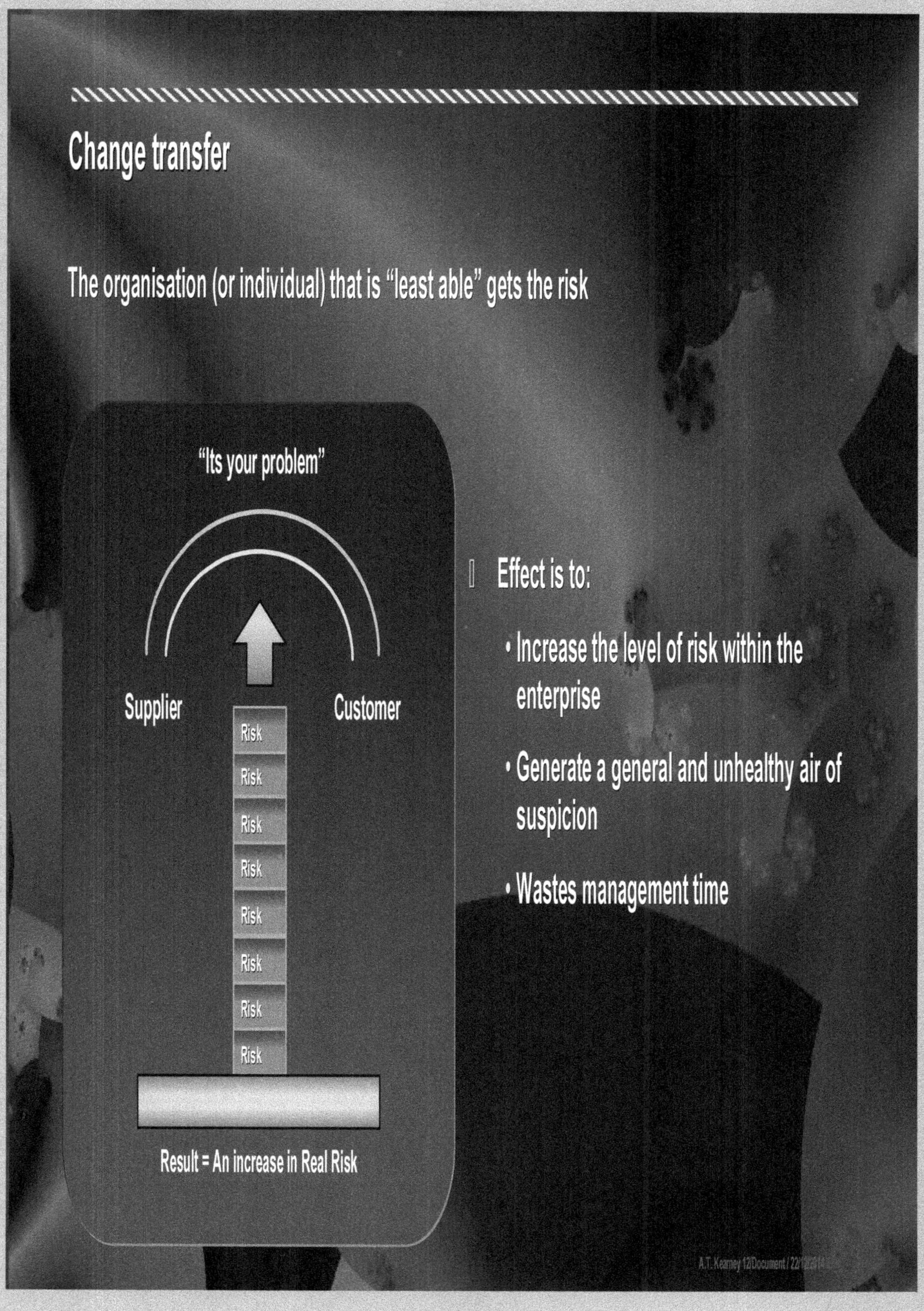
Change transfer
The organisation (or individual) that is "least able" gets the risk
"Its your problem"
Supplier
Customer
Risk
Risk
Risk
Risk
Risk
Risk
Risk
Risk
Result = An increase in Real Risk
Effect is to:
• Increase the level of risk within the enterprise
• Generate a general and unhealthy air of suspicion
• Wastes management time

Change transfer
Set up an open/joint process across the enterprise
"Its your problem"
Supplier
tomer
Risk
Risk
Risk
NO!
Result = An increase in Real Risk
Solution:
Involve all parties!
Only transfer when this results in a real reduction of risk to the enterprise

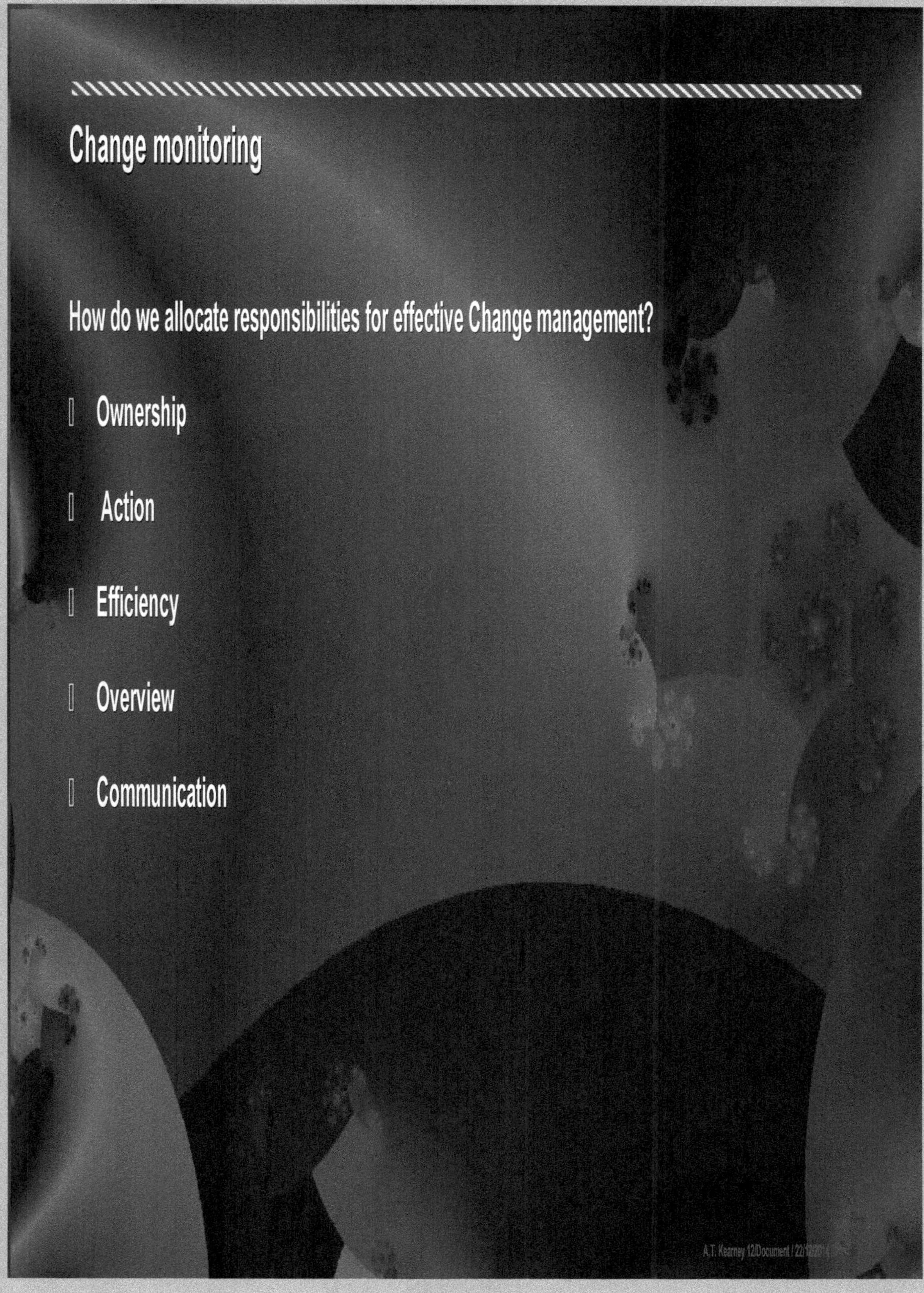

Change monitoring
How do we allocate responsibilities for effective Change management?
Ownership
Action
Efficiency
Overview
Communication
A.T. Kearney 12/Document

Change Monitoring

Traditional Change management responsibilities are often inefficient and confusing

- Change Owners are normally appointed who are responsible for the management of the Change
- A Change Manager is tasked with driving the process
- The Project Manager often owns many of the Changes

A.T. Kearney 12/Document / 22/12/2014

Change Monitoring

Traditional Change management responsibilities are often inefficient and confusing

- Change Owners are normally appointed who are responsible for the management of the Change –
  Result = Potential overload and lack of interest

- A Change Manager is tasked with driving the process –
  Result = Potentially seen as a low-value added role

- The Project Manager often owns many of the Changes –
  Result = The team transfer the risks to the PM!

A.T. Kearney 12/Document / 22/

Change Monitoring

Roles and Responsibilities

- Change Owner – The person who understands the Change best
- Change Action Manager – The person who will implement the action plan
- Project Manager – Oversees and drives the process
- Change Manager (Change Administrator) – Interviews and facilitates the process

A.T. Kearney 12/Document /

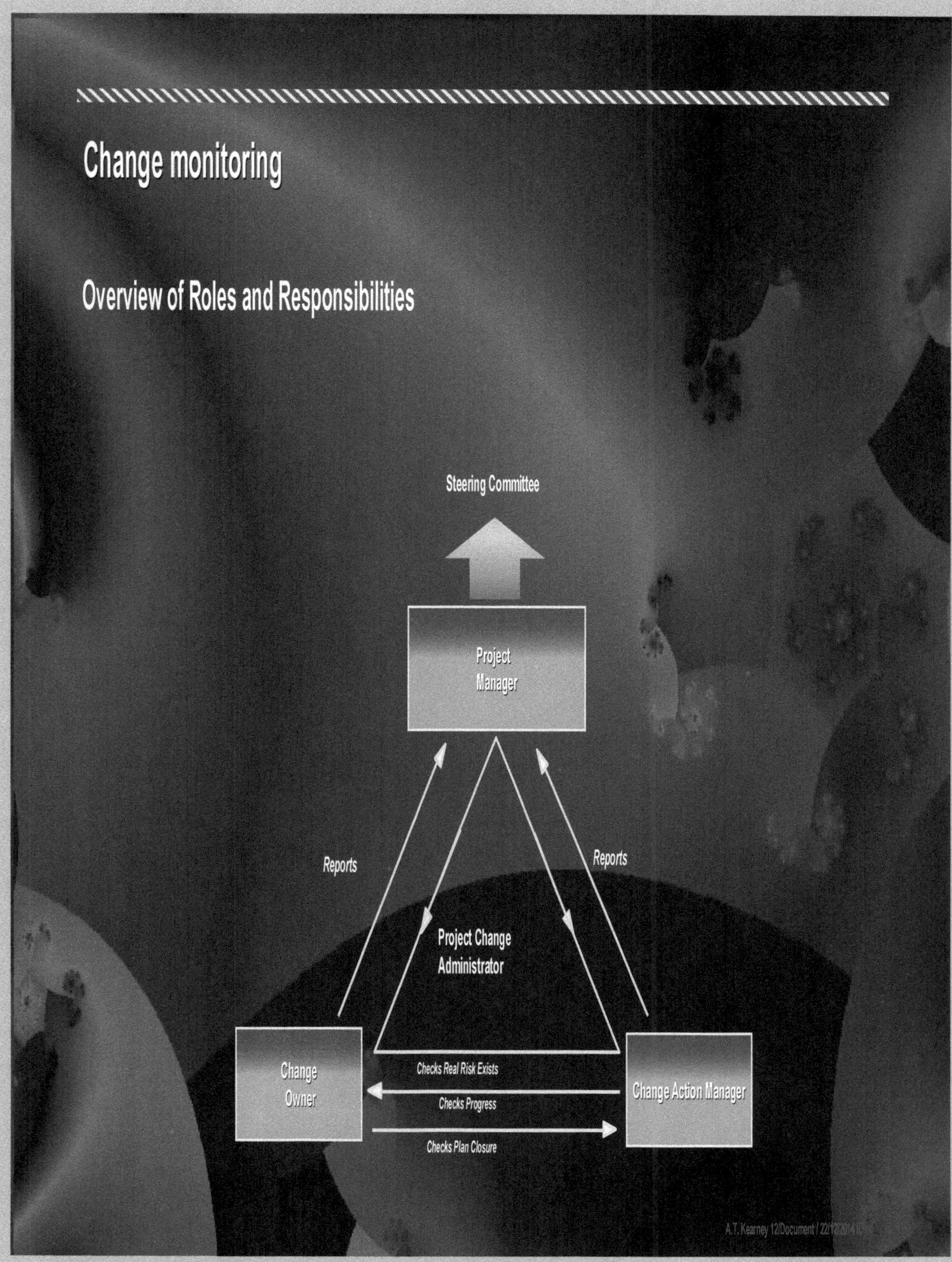
Change monitoring
Overview of Roles and Responsibilities
Steering Committee
Project Manager
Reports
Reports
Project Change Administrator
Change Owner
Checks Real Risk Exists
Change Action Manager
Checks Progress
Checks Plan Closure

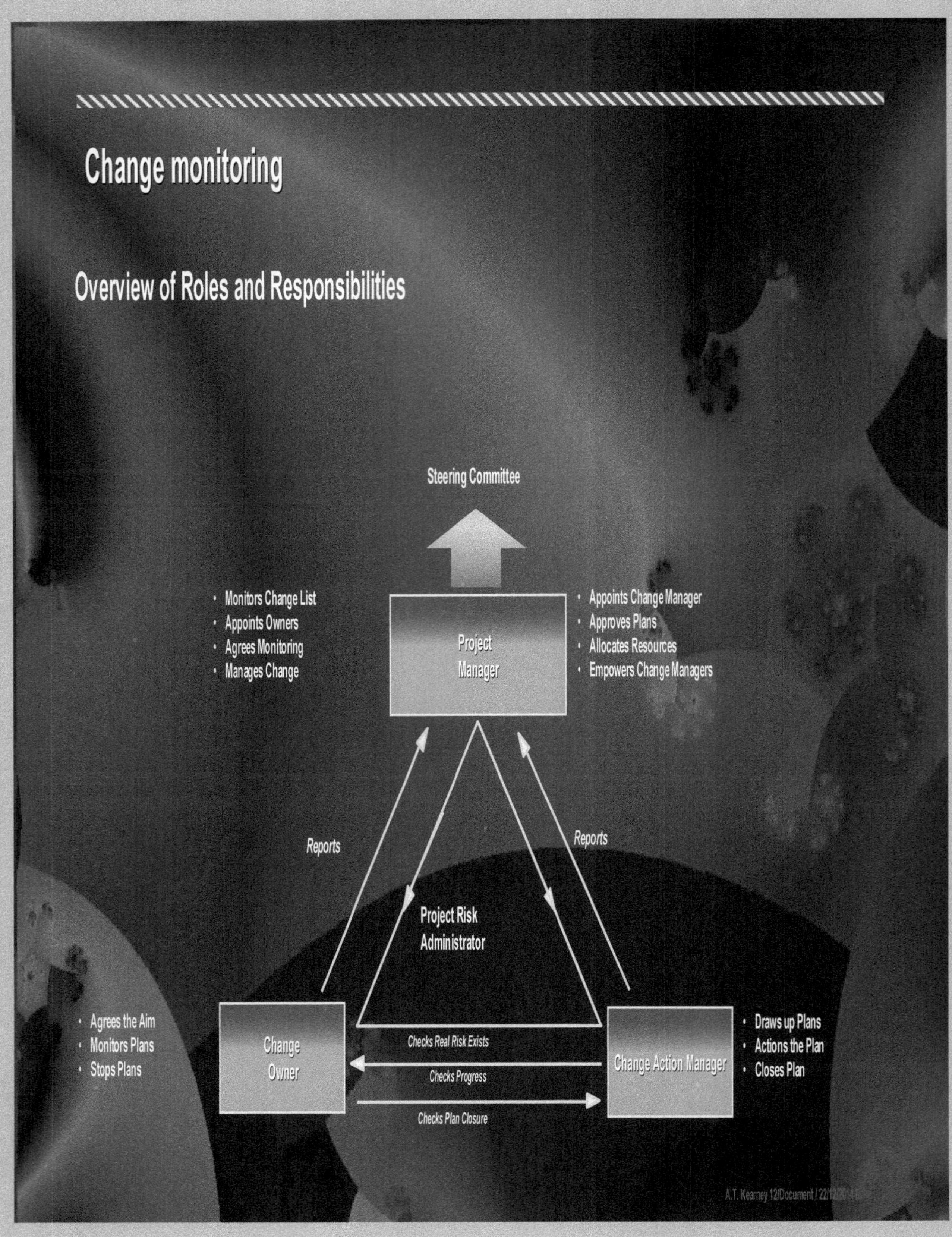
Change monitoring
Overview of Roles and Responsibilities
Steering Committee
Monitors Change List
Appoints Owners
Agrees Monitoring
Manages Change
Project Manager
Appoints Change Manager
Approves Plans
Allocates Resources
Empowers Change Managers
Reports
Reports
Project Risk Administrator
Agrees the Aim
Monitors Plans
Stops Plans
Change Owner
Checks Real Risk Exists
Checks Progress
Checks Plan Closure
Change Action Manager
Draws up Plans
Actions the Plan
Closes Plan

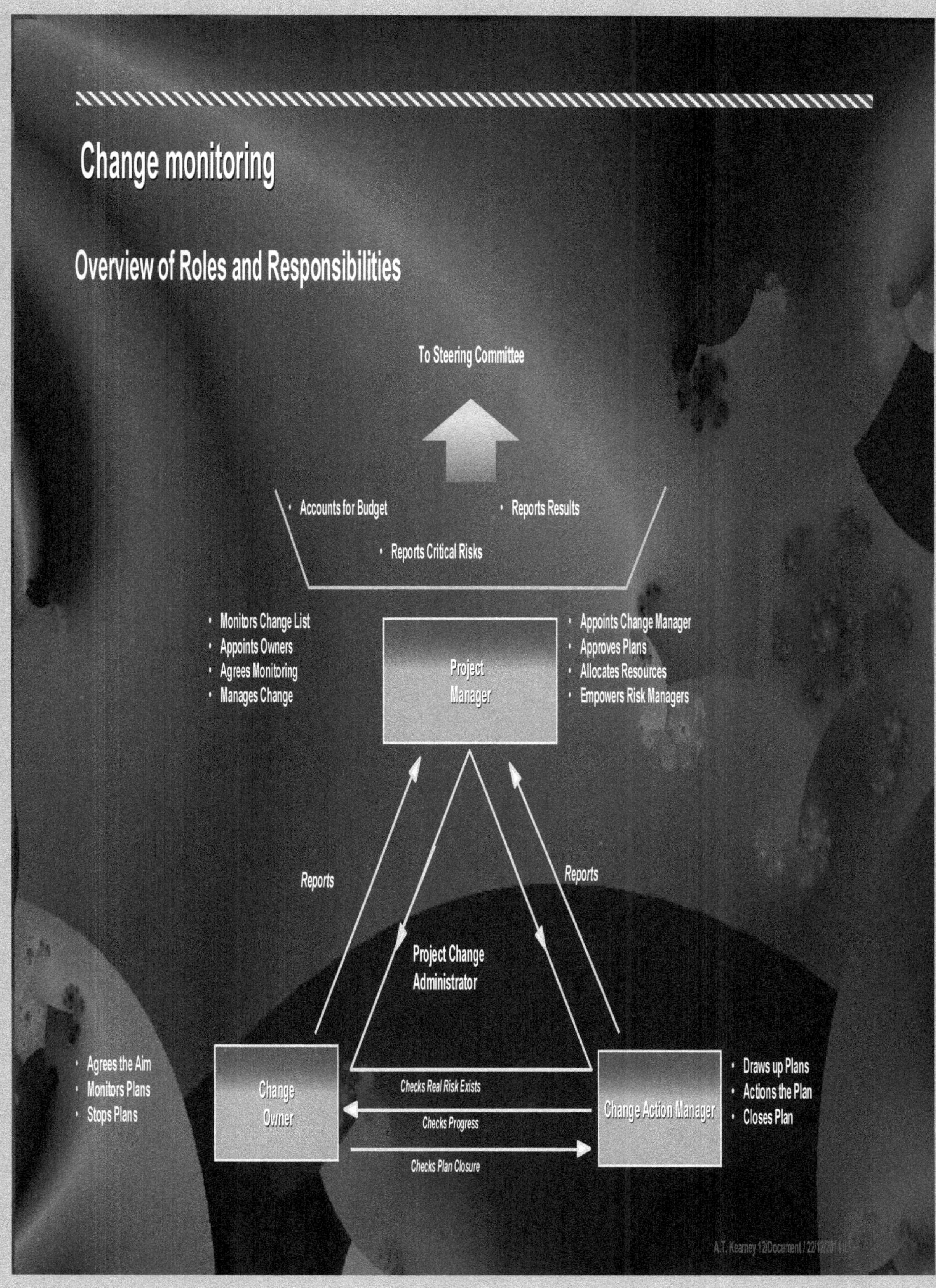
Change monitoring
Overview of Roles and Responsibilities
To Steering Committee
Accounts for Budget
Reports Results
Reports Critical Risks
Monitors Change List
Appoints Owners
Agrees Monitoring
Manages Change
Project Manager
Appoints Change Manager
Approves Plans
Allocates Resources
Empowers Risk Managers
Reports
Reports
Project Change Administrator
Agrees the Aim
Monitors Plans
Stops Plans
Change Owner
Checks Real Risk Exists
Checks Progress
Checks Plan Closure
Change Action Manager
Draws up Plans
Actions the Plan
Closes Plan

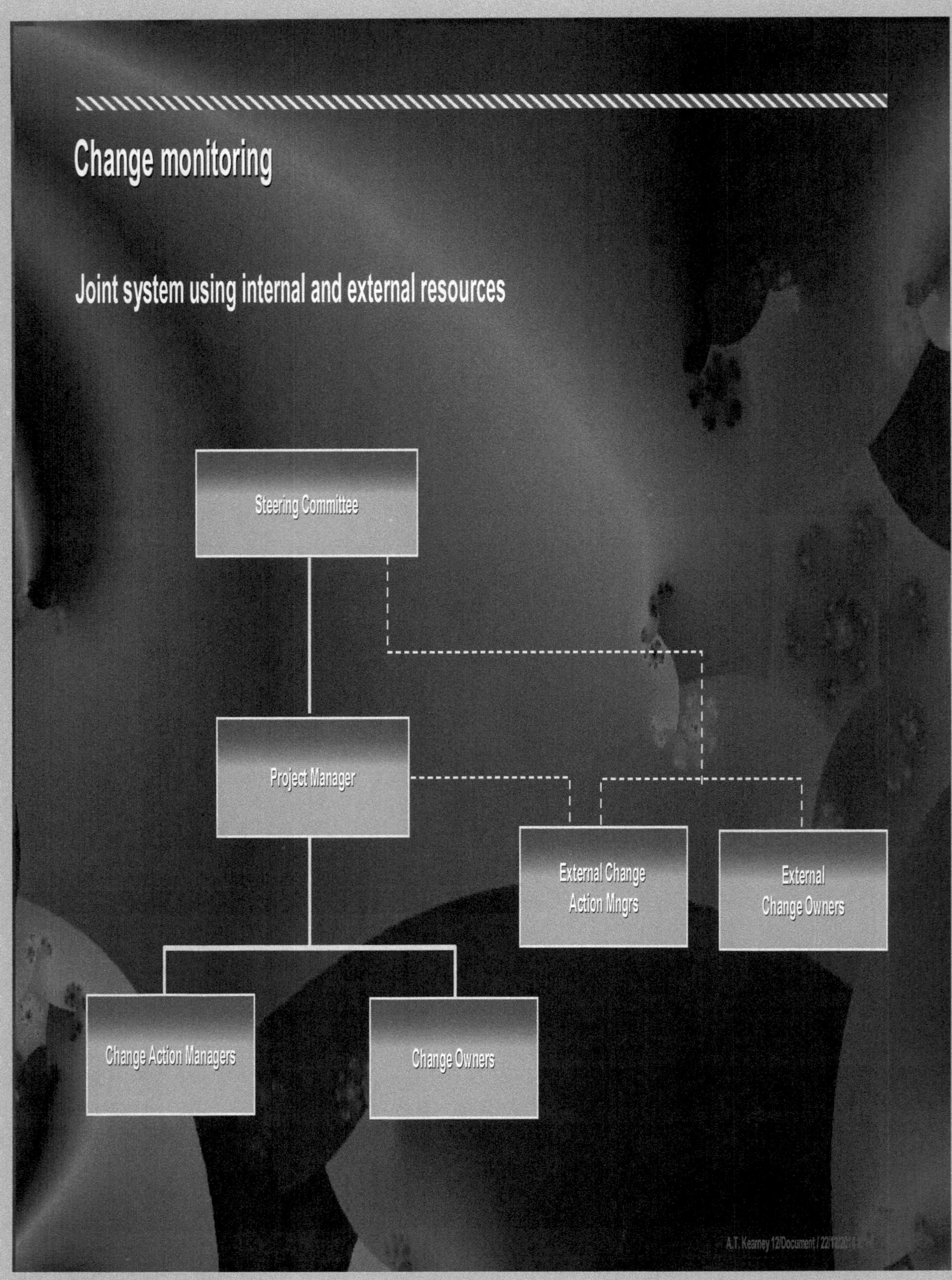
Change monitoring
Joint system using internal and external resources
Steering Committee
Project Manager
External Change Action Mngrs
External Change Owners
Change Action Managers
Change Owners
A.T. Kearney 12/Document /

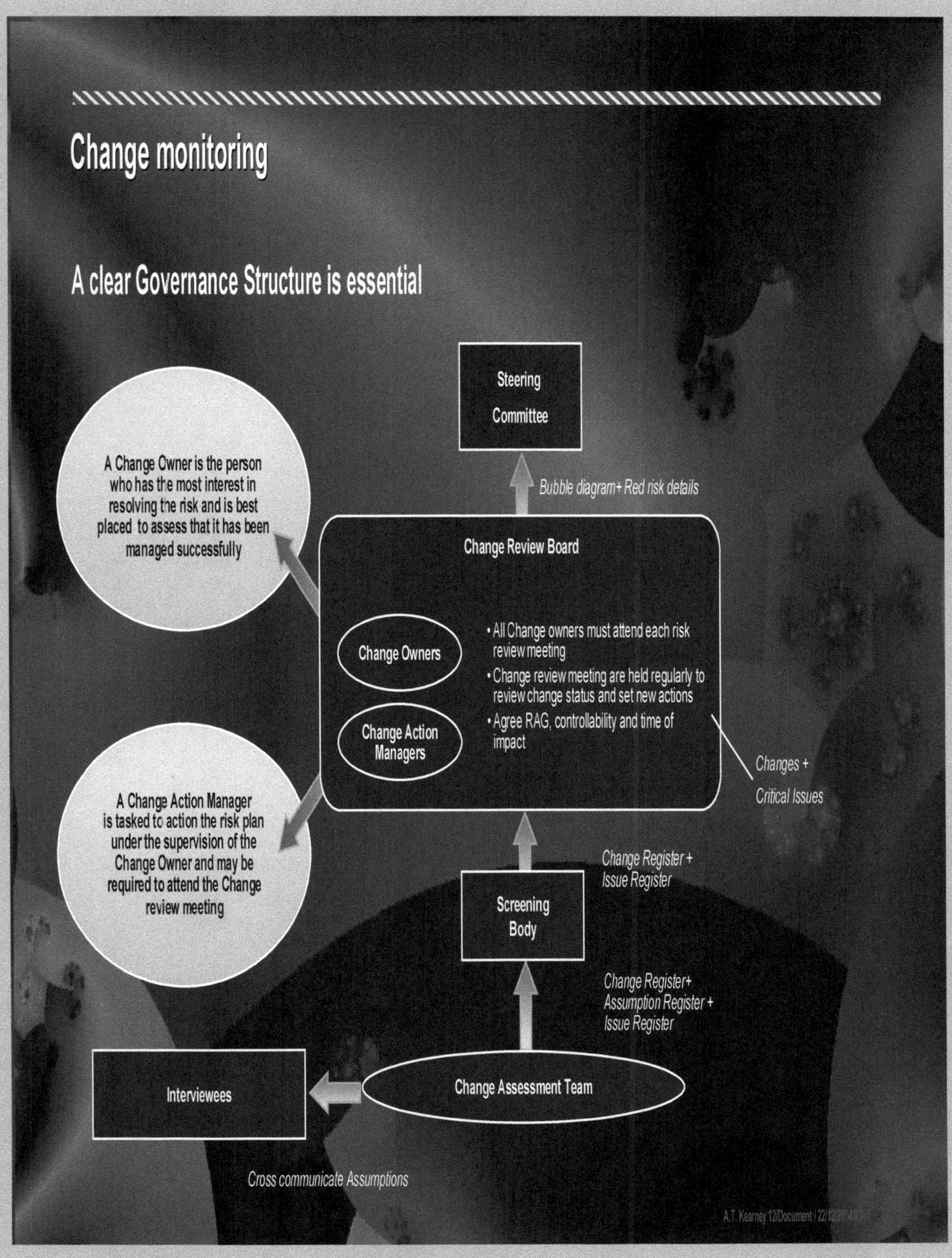
Change monitoring
A clear Governance Structure is essential
Steering
Committee
Bubble diagram+ Red risk details
A Change Owner is the person who has the most interest in resolving the risk and is best placed to assess that it has been managed successfully
Change Review Board
Change Owners
Change Action Managers
• All Change owners must attend each risk review meeting
• Change review meeting are held regularly to review change status and set new actions
• Agree RAG, controllability and time of impact
Changes +
Critical Issues
A Change Action Manager is tasked to action the risk plan under the supervision of the Change Owner and may be required to attend the Change review meeting
Change Register +
Issue Register
Screening
Body
Change Register+
Assumption Register +
Issue Register
Interviewees
Change Assessment Team
Cross communicate Assumptions

Change monitoring

Types of meetings and how often?

- Monthly Project Meetings
- Special Change Meetings
- Multi-level Change meetings
- Rolling process – BAD IDEA!

Change monitoring

Software tool support – Change Administration System (Change AS)

- Microsoft Access database tool
- Easy to use
- Generates Change Registers
- Automatic Bubble Diagrams

Remember: A fool with a tool is still a fool !

Project prioritisation
Why do we need to prioritise projects?
Some projects are more important or riskier than others
To ensure appropriate management attention
Deciding which projects to fund and resource
A.T. Kearney 12/Document / 22/12/2014

Project prioritisation

Prioritisation using Complexity and Criticality

- Business Criticality – How much does it matter if the project fails to meet its objectives (CSFs) A = nice to have, D = Critical to business
- Project Size – How much will the project (development and implementation) cost? A = smallest team, D = largest team
- Business Complexity – How many areas of the business will be involved in the project? A = one area, D = all/many areas
- Technical Complexity – How technically difficult is the project?
  A = simple/familiar technology/solution, D = new technology/scale never attempted etc

A.T. Kearney 12/Document / 22/12/2014

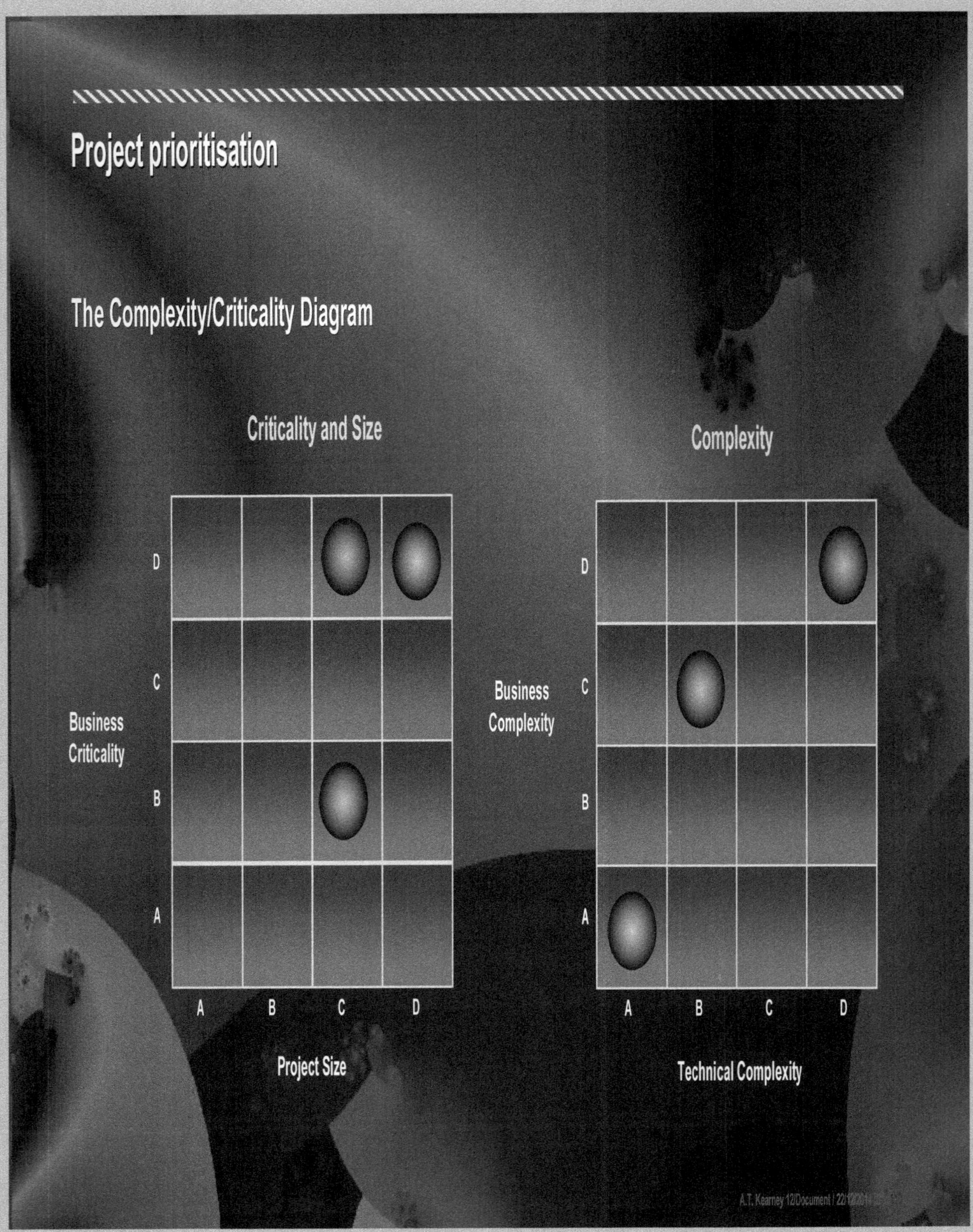
Project prioritisation
The Complexity/Criticality Diagram
Criticality and Size
Business Criticality
D
C
B
A
A
B
C
D
Project Size
Complexity
Business Complexity
D
C
B
A
A
B
C
D
Technical Complexity
A.T. Kearney 12/Document | 22/

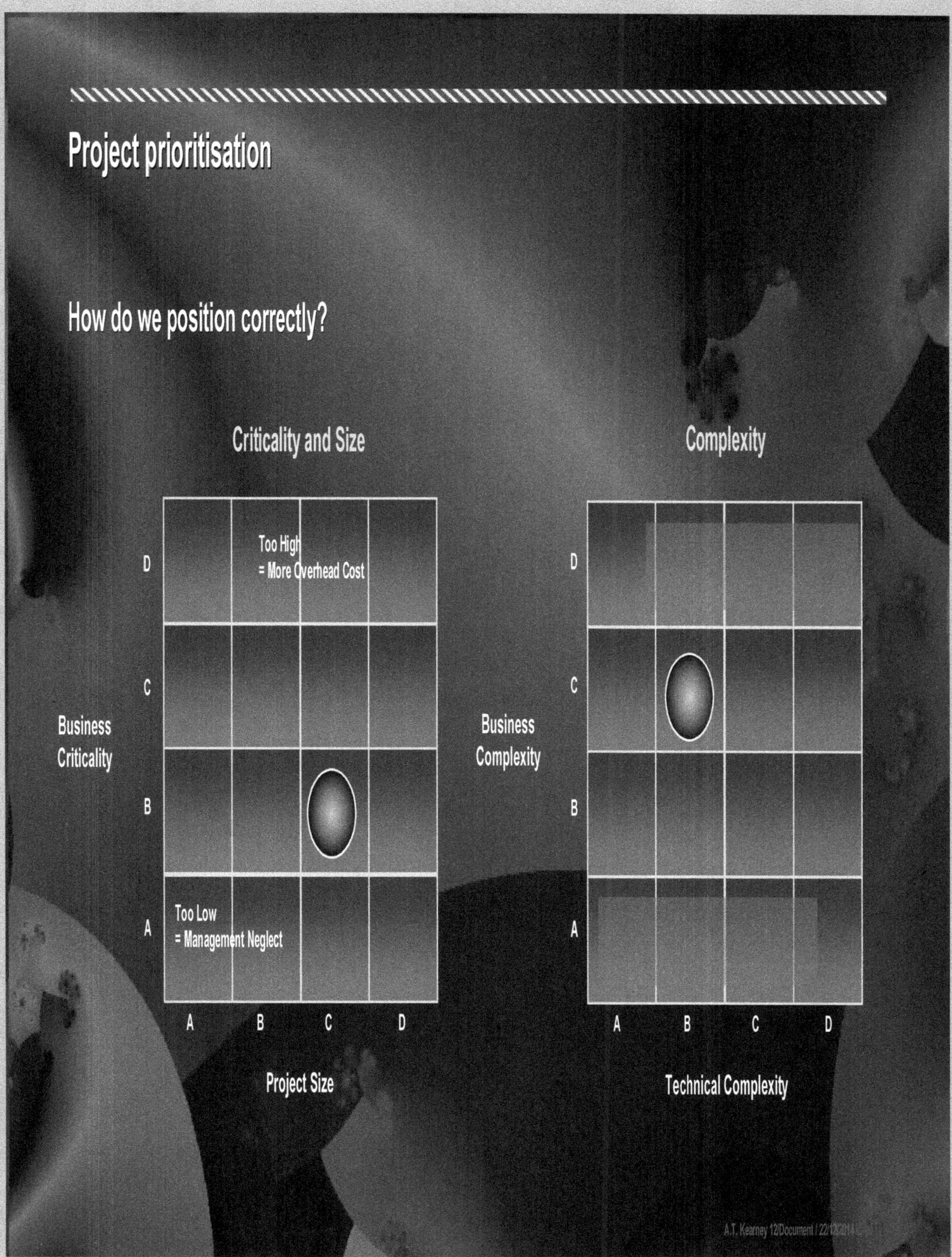
Project prioritisation
How do we position correctly?
Criticality and Size
Complexity
Too High
= More Overhead Cost
Too Low
= Management Neglect
Business
Criticality
Business
Complexity
D
C
B
A
A
B
C
D
Project Size
Technical Complexity

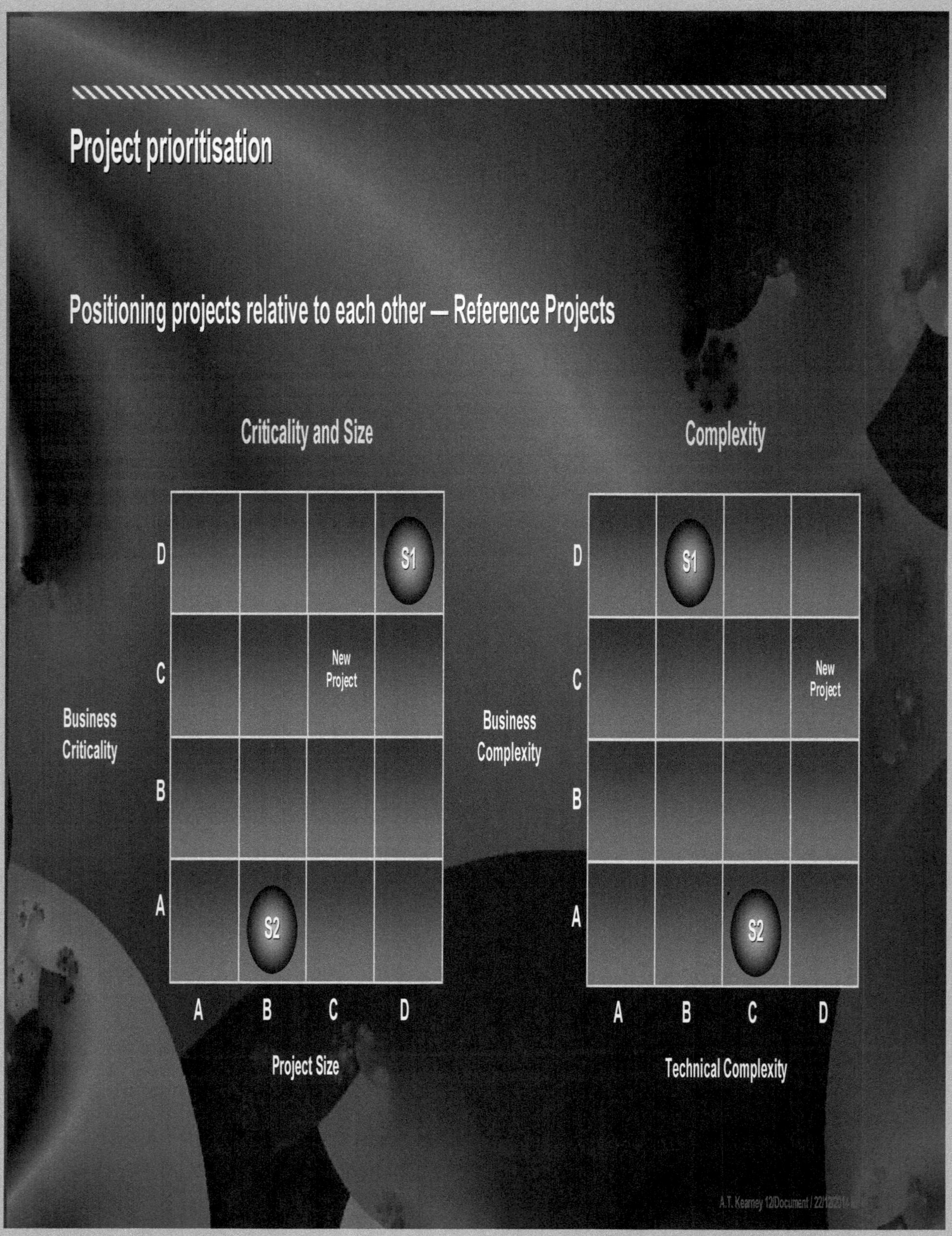

Project prioritisation
Positioning projects relative to each other – Reference Projects
Criticality and Size
Complexity
Business Criticality
D
C
B
A
S1
New Project
S2
A
B
C
D
Project Size
Business Complexity
D
C
B
A
S1
New Project
S2
A
B
C
D
Technical Complexity
A.T. Kearney 12/Document

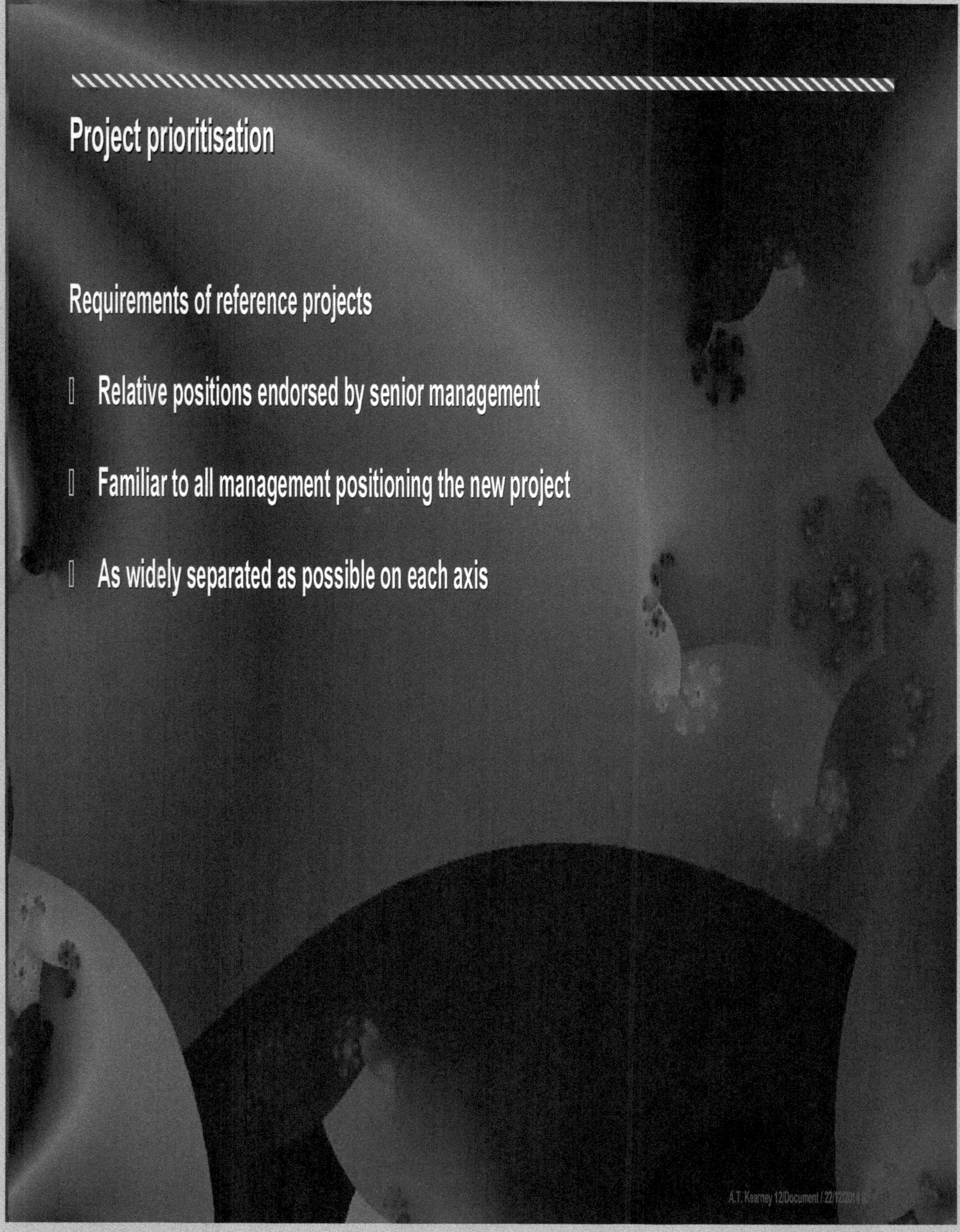
Project prioritisation
Requirements of reference projects
Relative positions endorsed by senior management
Familiar to all management positioning the new project
As widely separated as possible on each axis

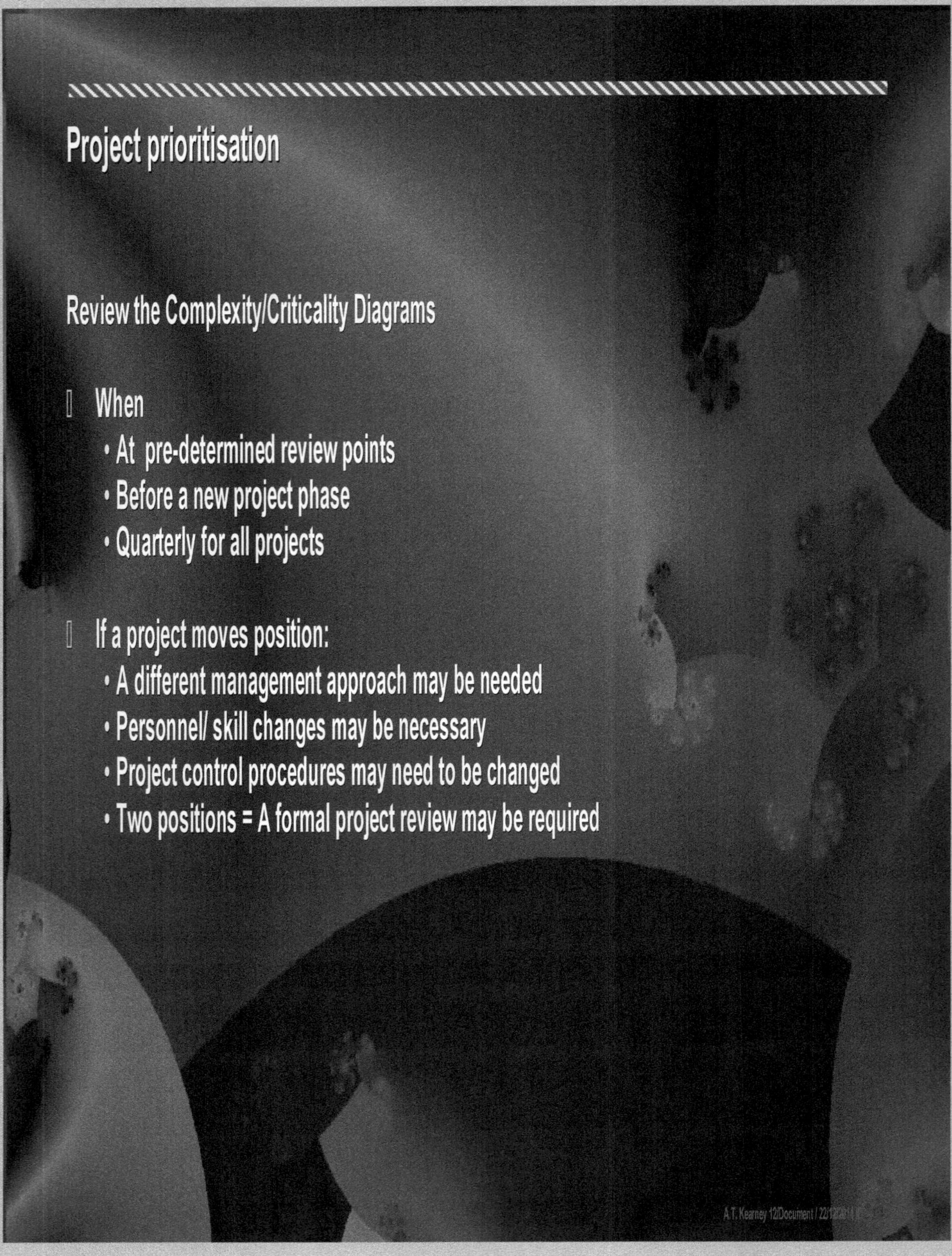
Project prioritisation
Review the Complexity/Criticality Diagrams
When
• At pre-determined review points
• Before a new project phase
• Quarterly for all projects
If a project moves position:
• A different management approach may be needed
• Personnel/ skill changes may be necessary
• Project control procedures may need to be changed
• Two positions = A formal project review may be required

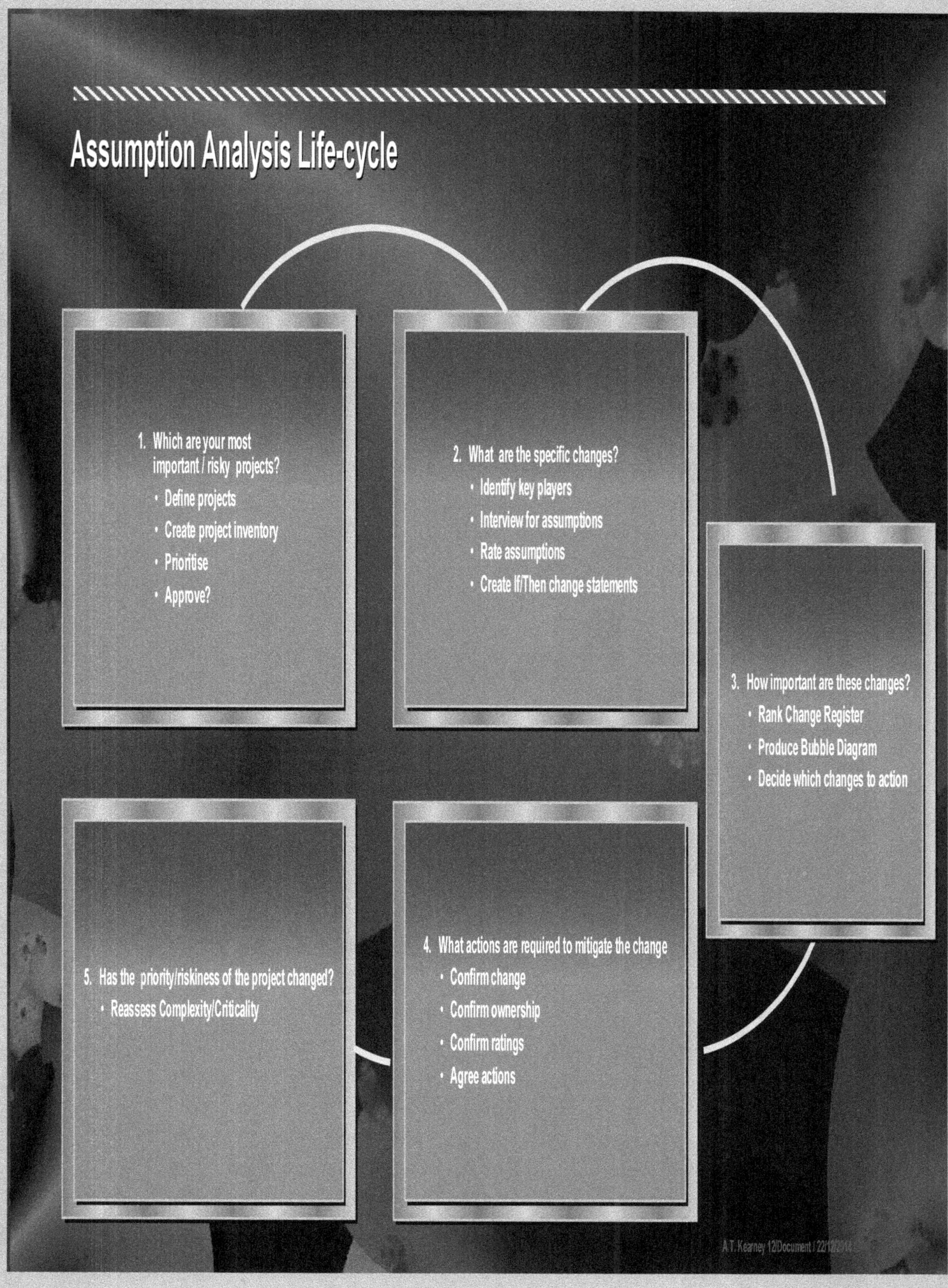
Assumption Analysis Life-cycle
1. Which are your most important / risky projects?
• Define projects
• Create project inventory
• Prioritise
• Approve?
2. What are the specific changes?
• Identify key players
• Interview for assumptions
• Rate assumptions
• Create If/Then change statements
3. How important are these changes?
• Rank Change Register
• Produce Bubble Diagram
• Decide which changes to action
4. What actions are required to mitigate the change
• Confirm change
• Confirm ownership
• Confirm ratings
• Agree actions
5. Has the priority/riskiness of the project changed?
• Reassess Complexity/Criticality
A.T. Kearney 12/Document

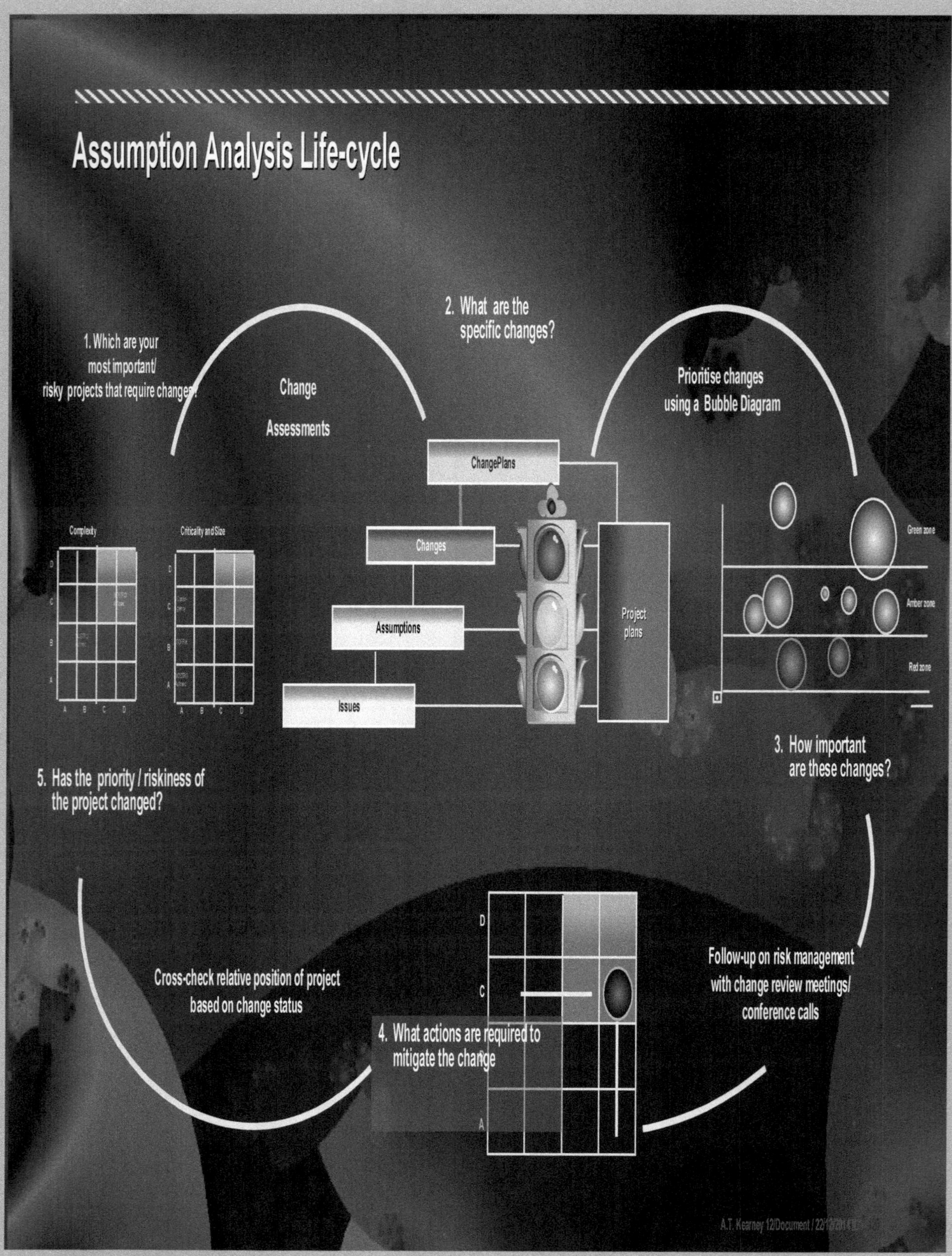
Assumption Analysis Life-cycle
1. Which are your most important/ risky projects that require changes?
Change Assessments
2. What are the specific changes?
Prioritise changes using a Bubble Diagram
ChangePlans
Changes
Assumptions
Issues
Project plans
Complexity
Criticality and Size
Green zone
Amber zone
Red zone
3. How important are these changes?
5. Has the priority / riskiness of the project changed?
Cross-check relative position of project based on change status
4. What actions are required to mitigate the change
Follow-up on risk management with change review meetings/ conference calls

Conclusions

Adopting change management methods

- Any "true" change management method is better than none
- The methodology explained in Change Management In I.T. book addresses the deficiencies in traditional methods
- Change Management In I.T. works!!

Conclusions
Which projects benefit most from Change Management In I.T. ?
Large projects (many resources)
Complex projects
Multi-country or Global projects
Multiple Projects and Programmes
Tight timeframes
Must do!

Conclusions

Who in the organisation will see the benefits of Change Management In I.T. clearly?

- Head of the organization = CEO?
- One step down = CFO/CIO?
- Programme Director
- Project Manager

Depends on the role and management style of the management team

Hands on - hard sell

Hands off - easy sell

Conclusions

Where does **Change Management In I.T.** fit into project management?

- Planning
- Resource Management
- Personnel Management
- Configuration Management
- Change Control
- Quality Management
- Financial Control
- Contract Management
- Business Management and Administration

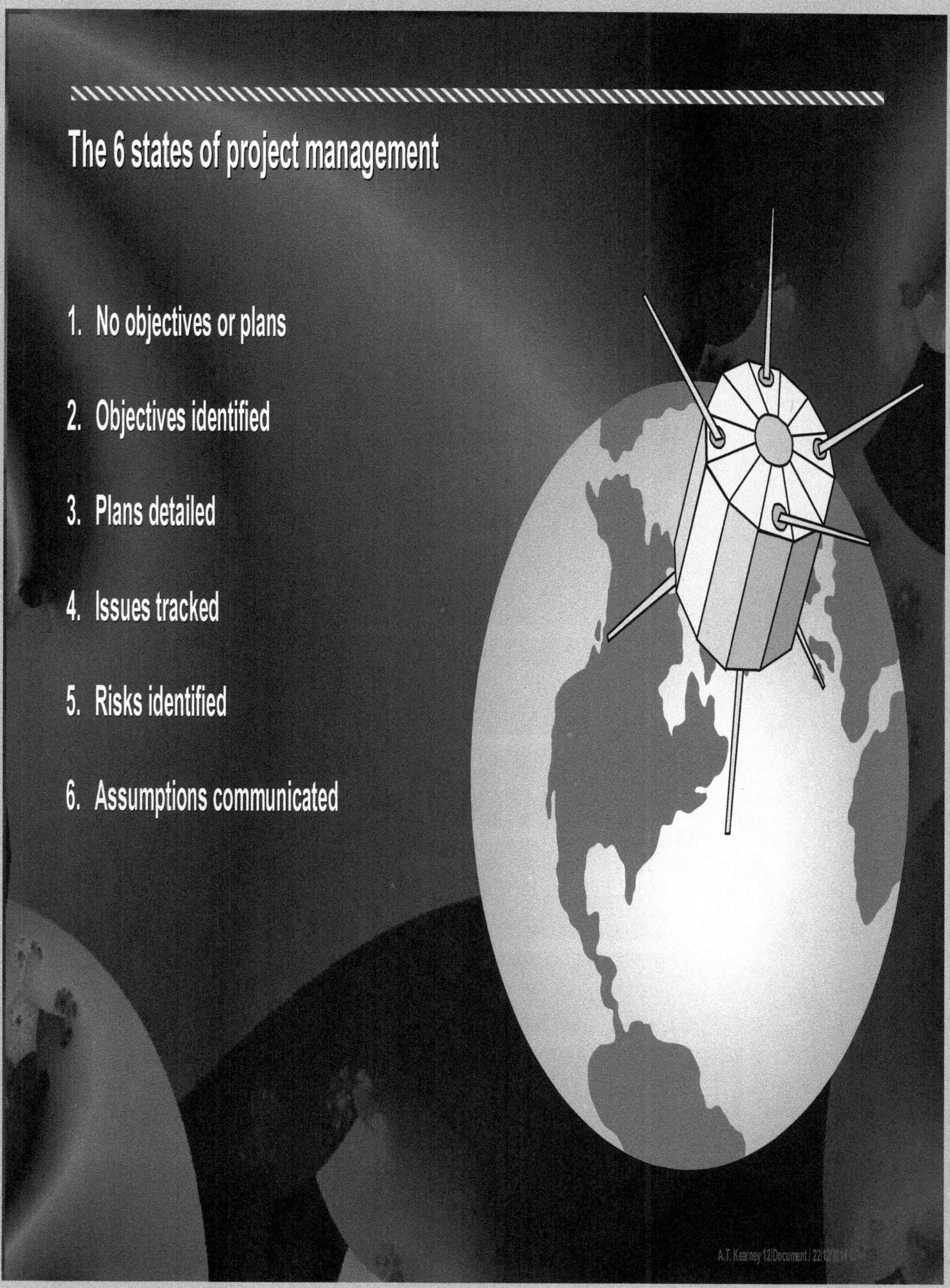
The 6 states of project management
1. No objectives or plans
2. Objectives identified
3. Plans detailed
4. Issues tracked
5. Risks identified
6. Assumptions communicated
A.T. Kearney 12/Document /

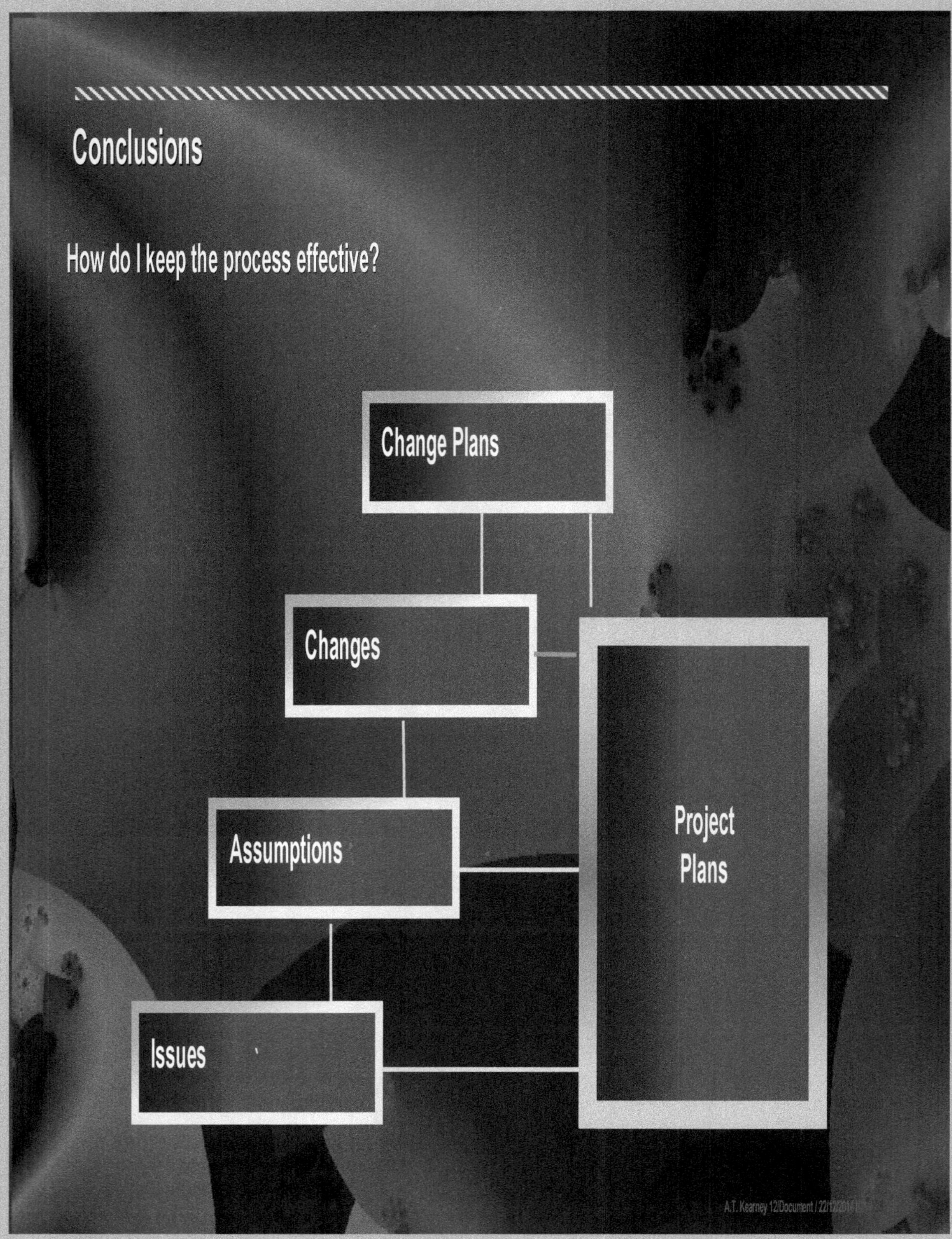
Conclusions
How do I keep the process effective?
Change Plans
Changes
Assumptions
Issues
Project
Plans

Conclusions
How do I keep the process effective?
Change Plans
Changes
Assumptions
Issues
Project Plans
The process must be forward looking
A.T. Kearney 12/Document

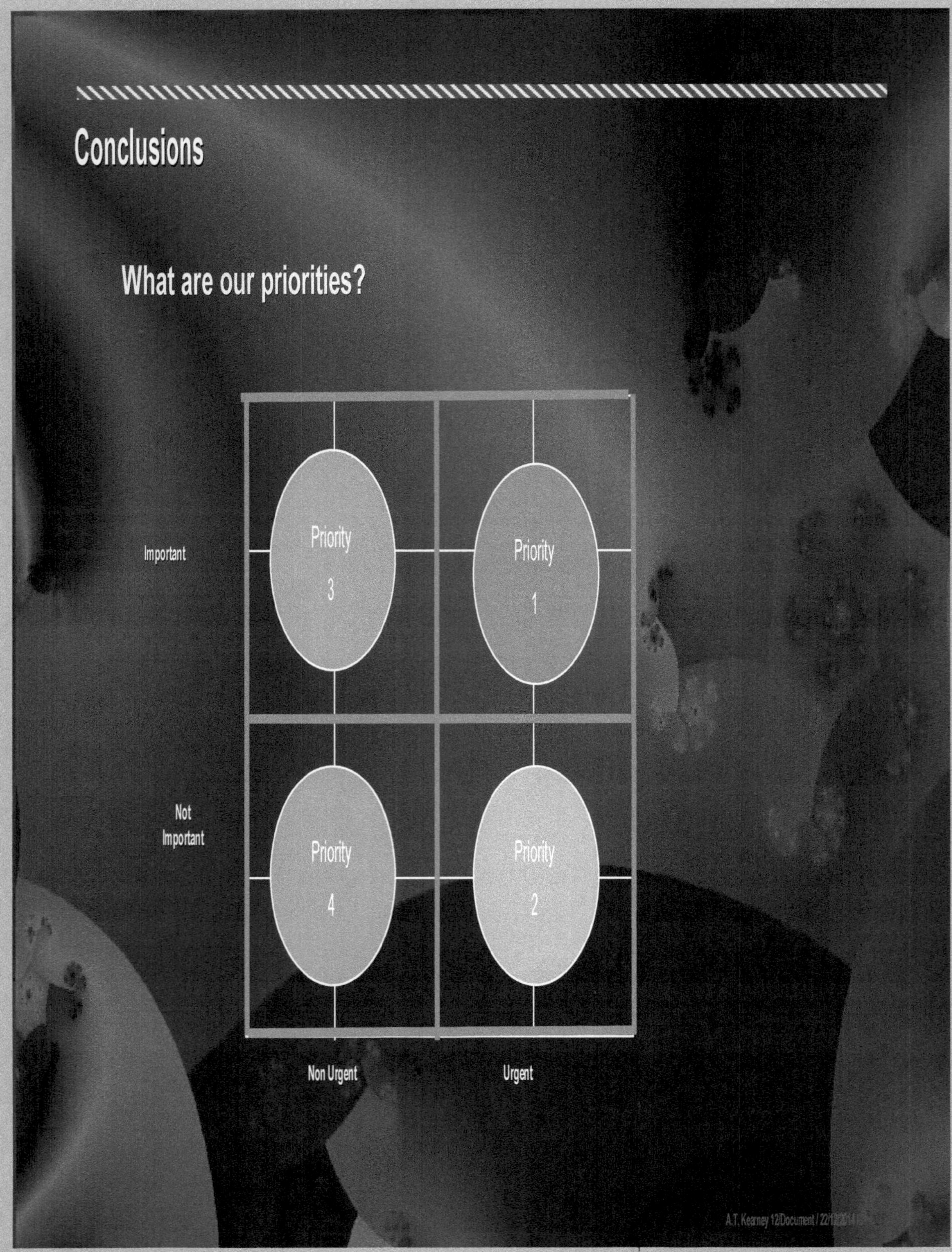
Conclusions
What are our priorities?
Important
Not
Important
Priority
3
Priority
1
Priority
4
Priority
2
Non Urgent
Urgent

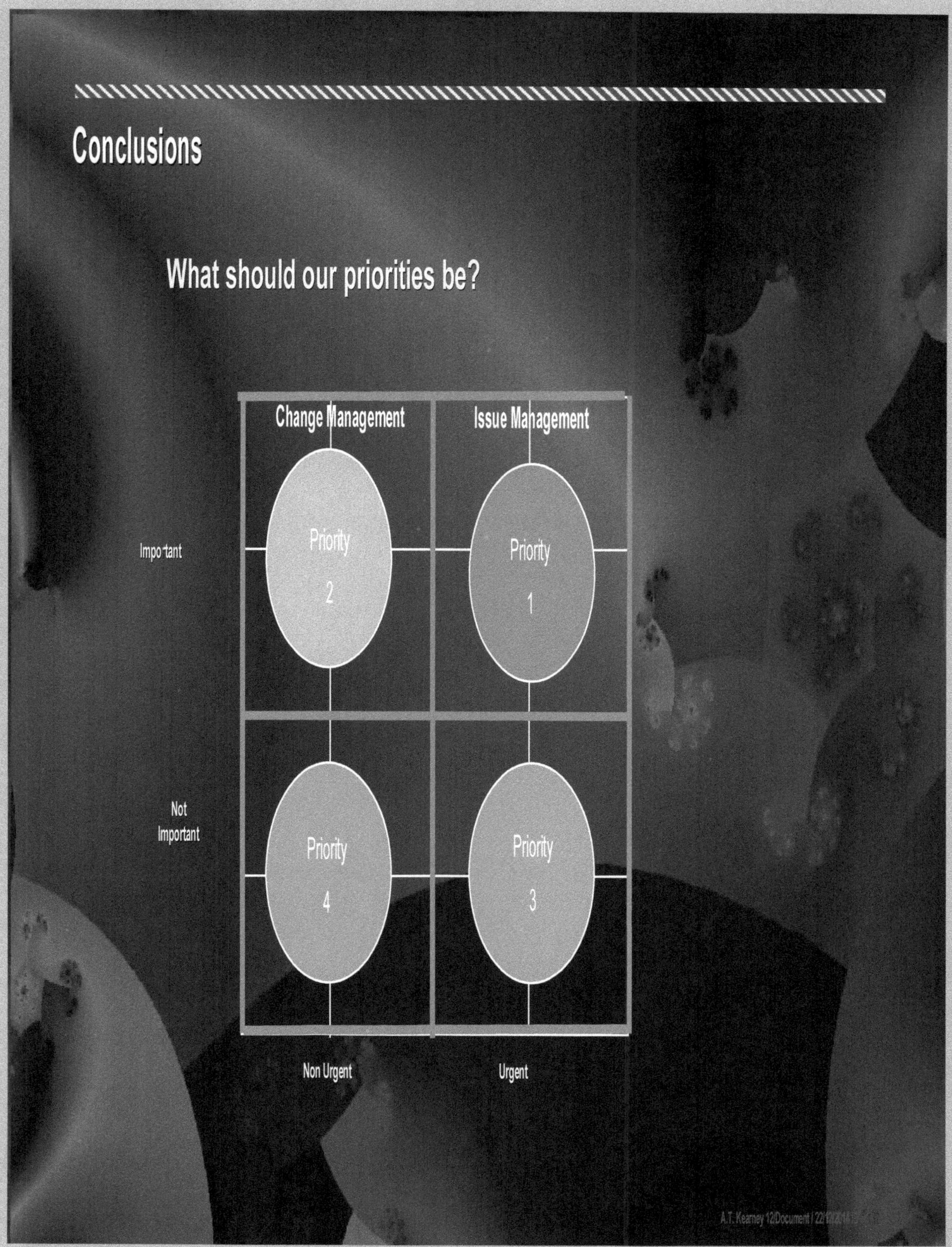
Conclusions
What should our priorities be?
Change Management
Issue Management
Important
Not Important
Priority 2
Priority 1
Priority 4
Priority 3
Non Urgent
Urgent

Conclusions
What to look out for...
Capturing the "wrong" assumption
Ensure that the consequences pass the "so-what" test
Action roll-over
Obtaining the right level of ownership

Change Management In I.T. philosophy

Before Change Management In I.T. concepts

Supplier: "I think we have a million dollar problem!"

Purchaser: "What's all this "we" rubbish? You said that you would deliver..."

After Change Management In I.T. methodology

Supplier: "Do you realise the current plans are based on a DD assumption?"

Purchaser: "Oh really? What can we do about it?"

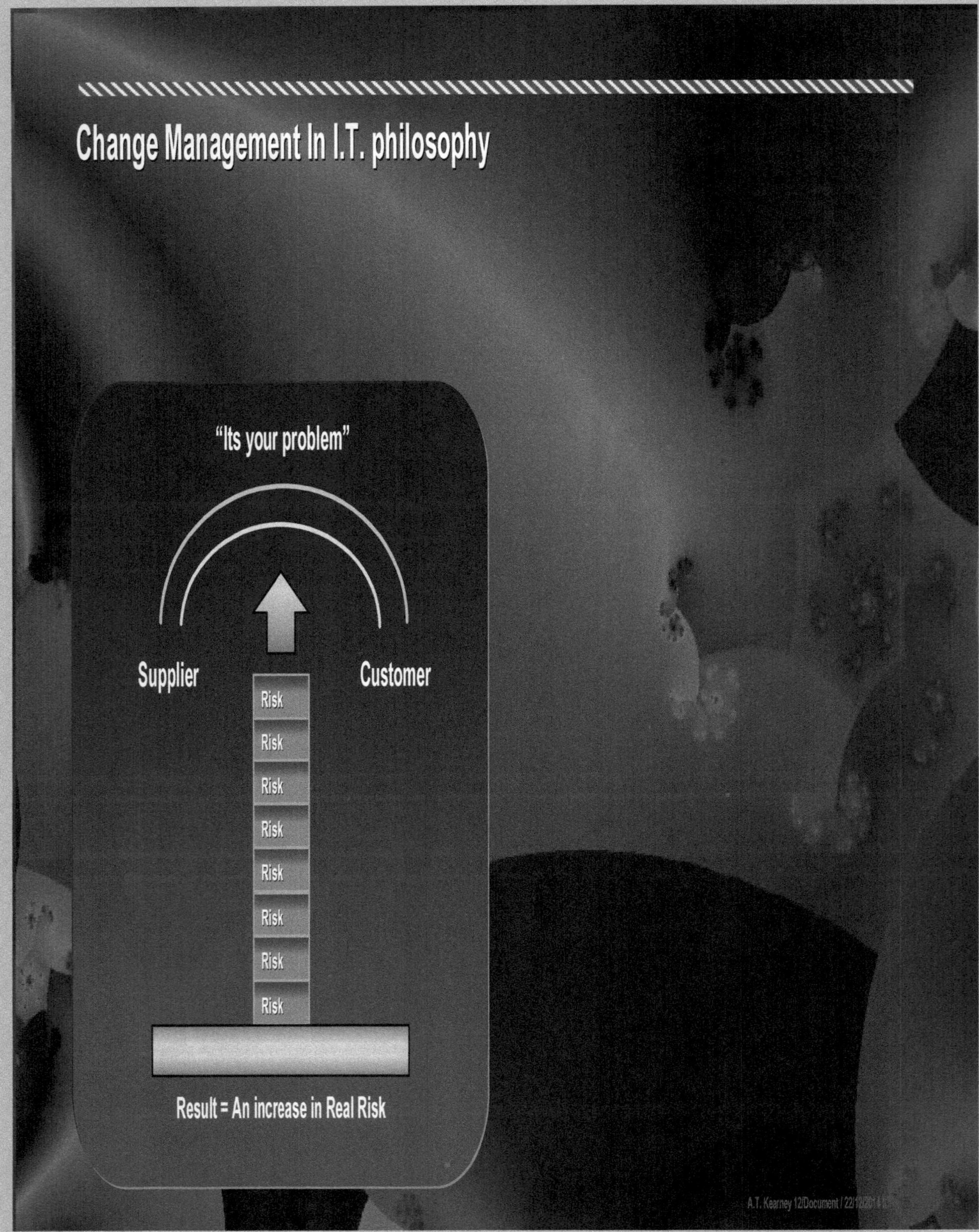
Change Management In I.T. philosophy
"Its your problem"
Supplier
Customer
Risk
Risk
Risk
Risk
Risk
Risk
Risk
Risk
Result = An increase in Real Risk

Establishing project costs
Normal estimating techniques mix the good and poor quality data – ie Single point estimate
Probability
Add Up
Cost
Cost $

Change identification – Strategic Cost Analysis

The project Brick Wall contains all project cost elements

- Vertical Bricks are one offs – they occur at a certain point in the project (e.g. to implement a piece of software is a Vertical Brick)
- Horizontal Bricks continue throughout the project (e.g. Project Management is a Horizontal Brick)
- Total project cost is signified by a complete "Brick Wall"

A.T. Kearney 12/Document / 22/

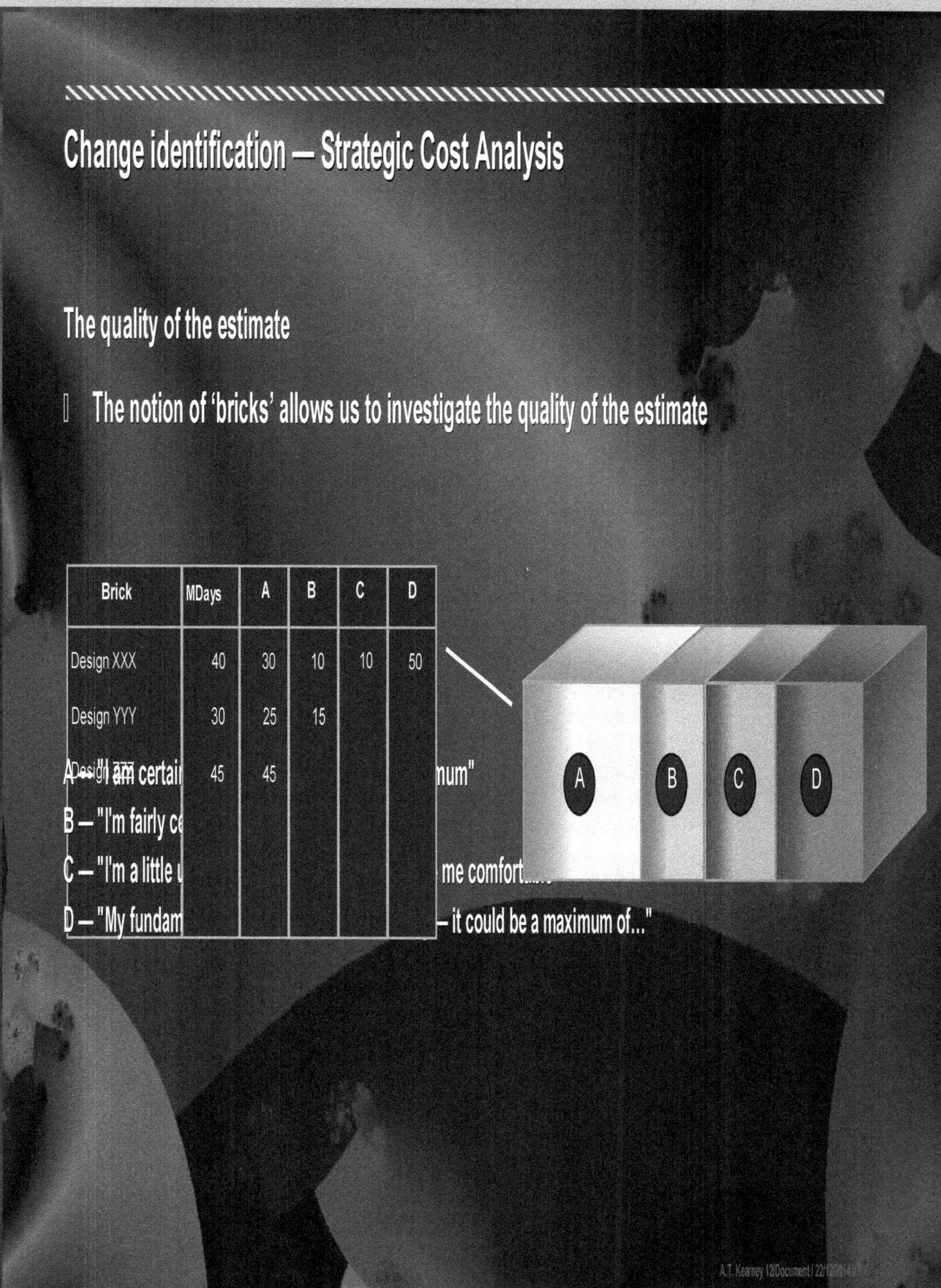

Brick	MDays	A	B	C	D
Design XXX	40	30	10	10	50
Design YYY	30	25	15		
Design ZZZ	45	45			

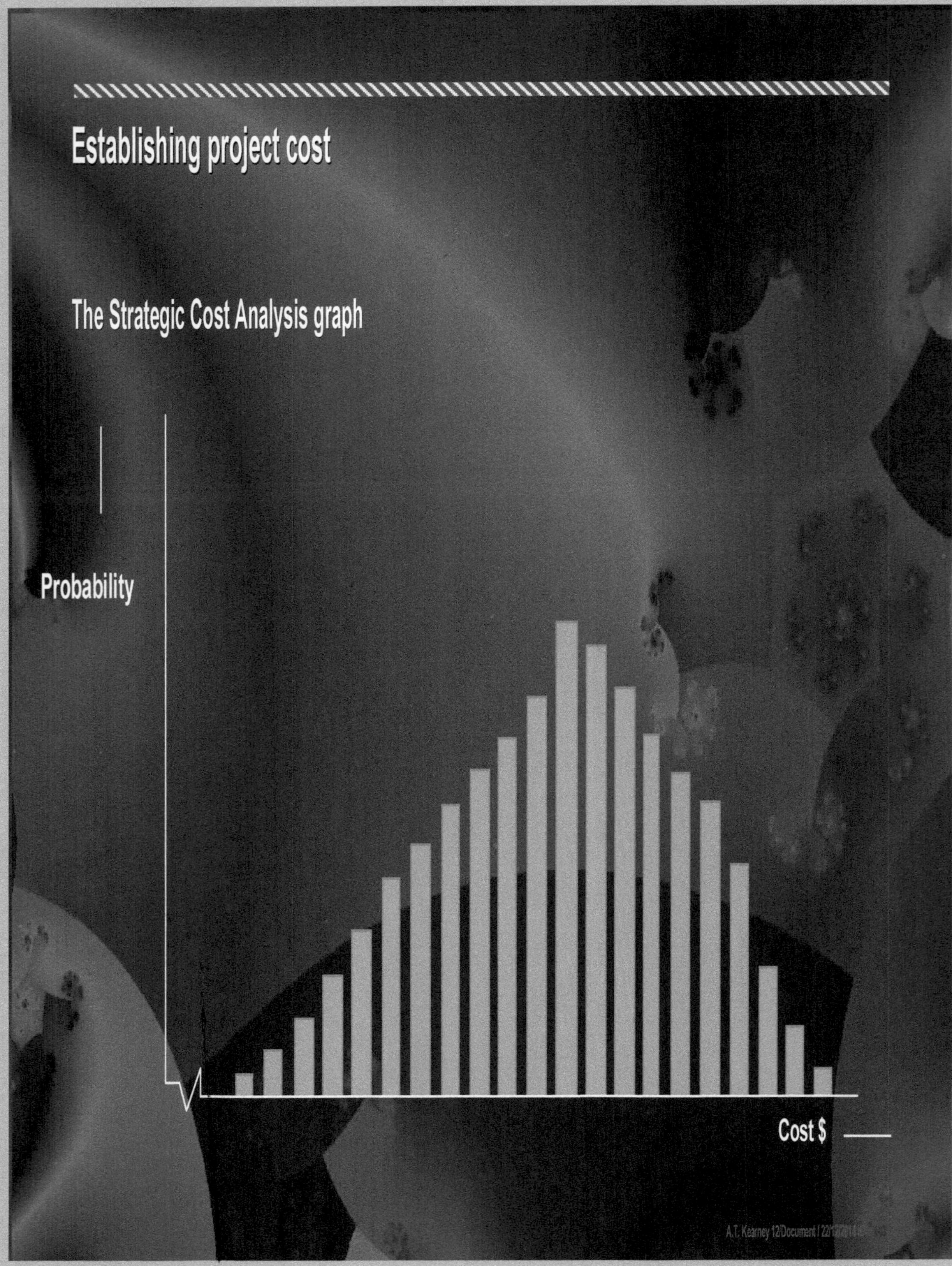
Establishing project cost
The Strategic Cost Analysis graph
Probability
Cost $
A.T. Kearney 12/Document

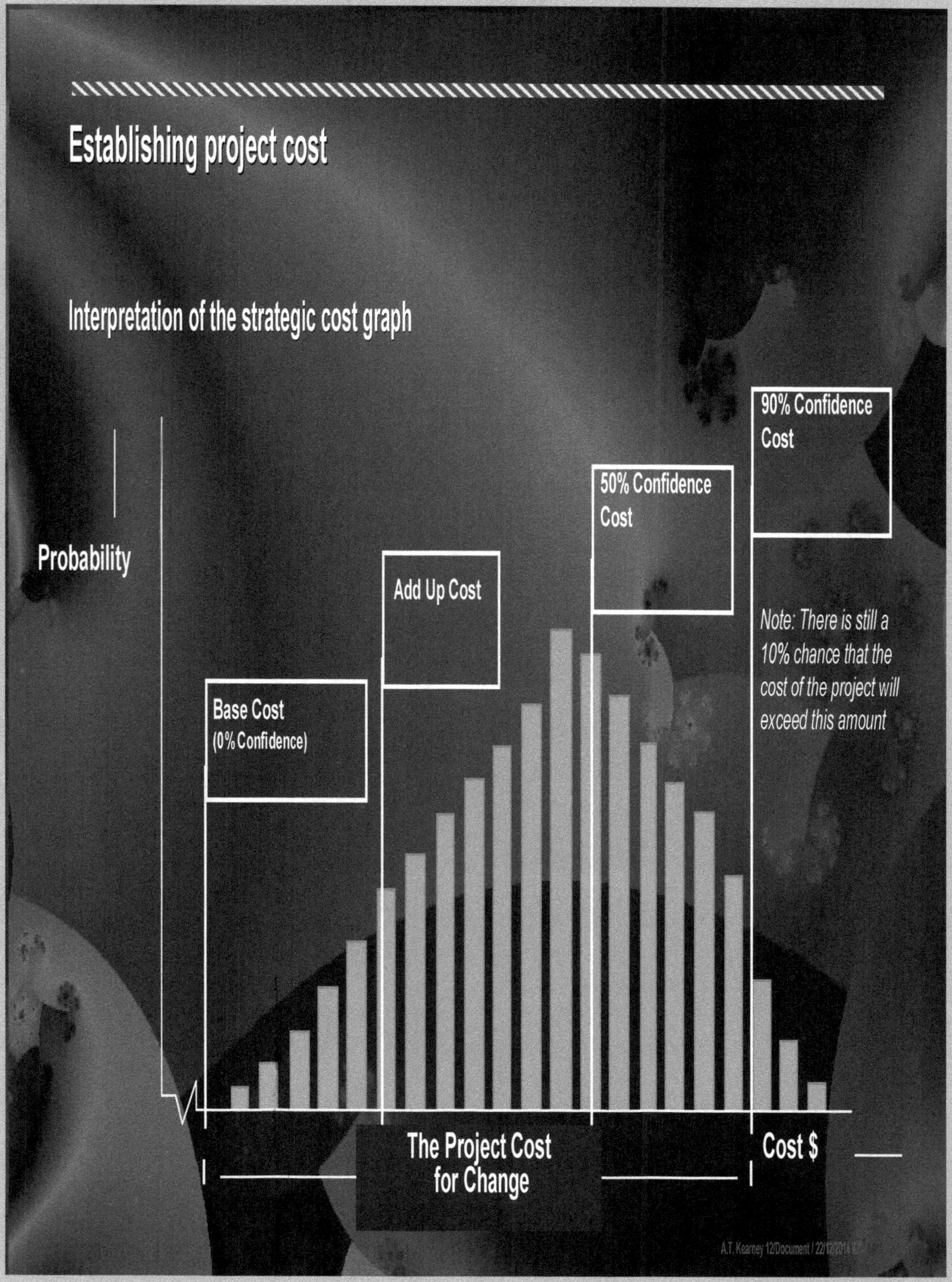
Establishing project cost
Interpretation of the strategic cost graph
Probability
Base Cost
(0% Confidence)
Add Up Cost
50% Confidence
Cost
90% Confidence
Cost
Note: There is still a
10% chance that the
cost of the project will
exceed this amount
The Project Cost
for Change
Cost $

Change identification

Strategic cost analysis

- Refines normal approaches to cost estimating
- Helps to quantify total cost uncertainty in a project
- Encourages objective contingency budget setting
- Can be used in difficult price negotiations
- Allows a risk budget approach
- Kick-starts the risk assessment process

A.T. Kearney 12/Document / 22/12/2014

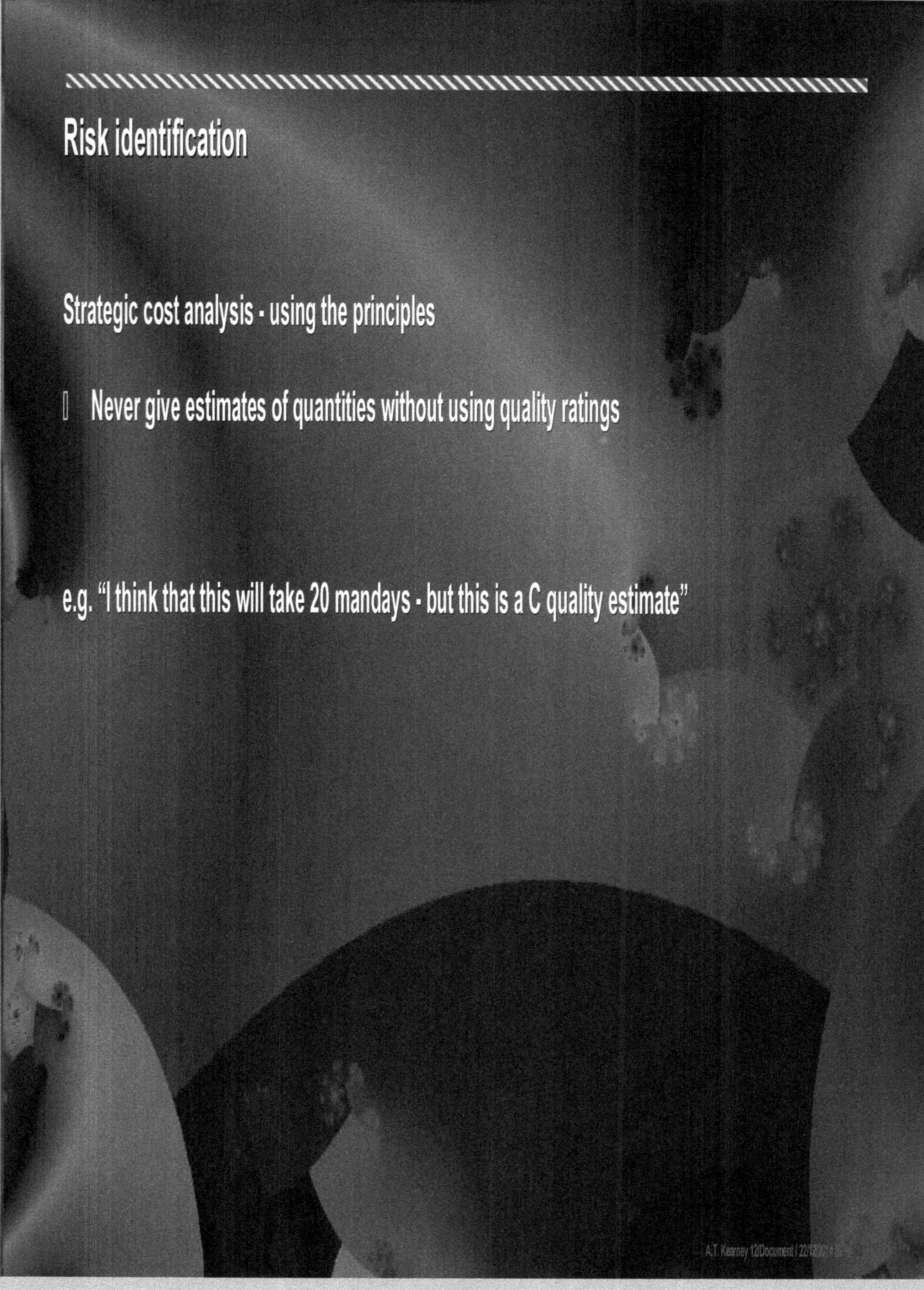
Risk identification
Strategic cost analysis - using the principles
Never give estimates of quantities without using quality ratings
e.g. “I think that this will take 20 mandays - but this is a C quality estimate”

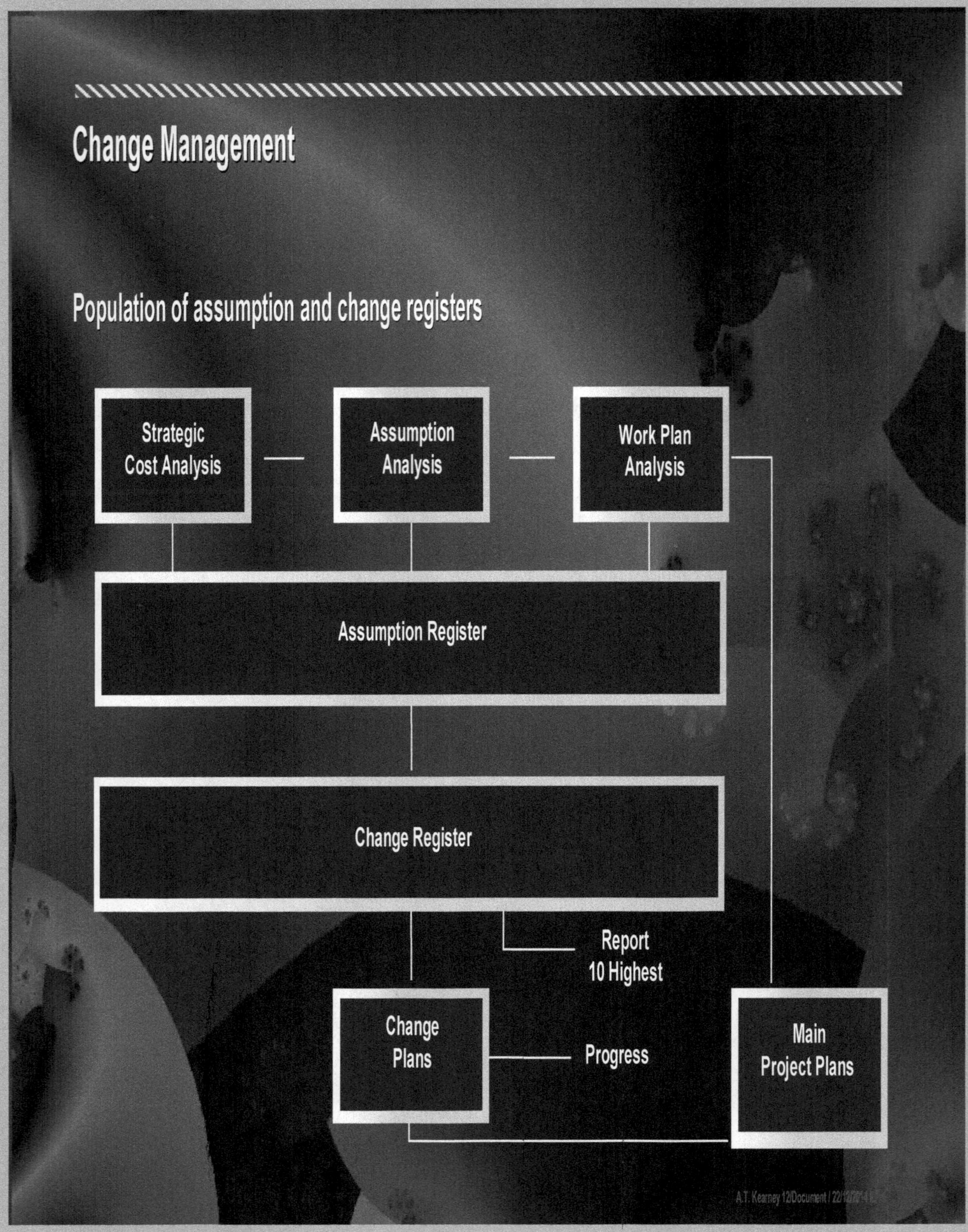
Change Management
Population of assumption and change registers
Strategic Cost Analysis
Assumption Analysis
Work Plan Analysis
Assumption Register
Change Register
Report 10 Highest
Change Plans
Progress
Main Project Plans
A.T. Kearney 12/Document /

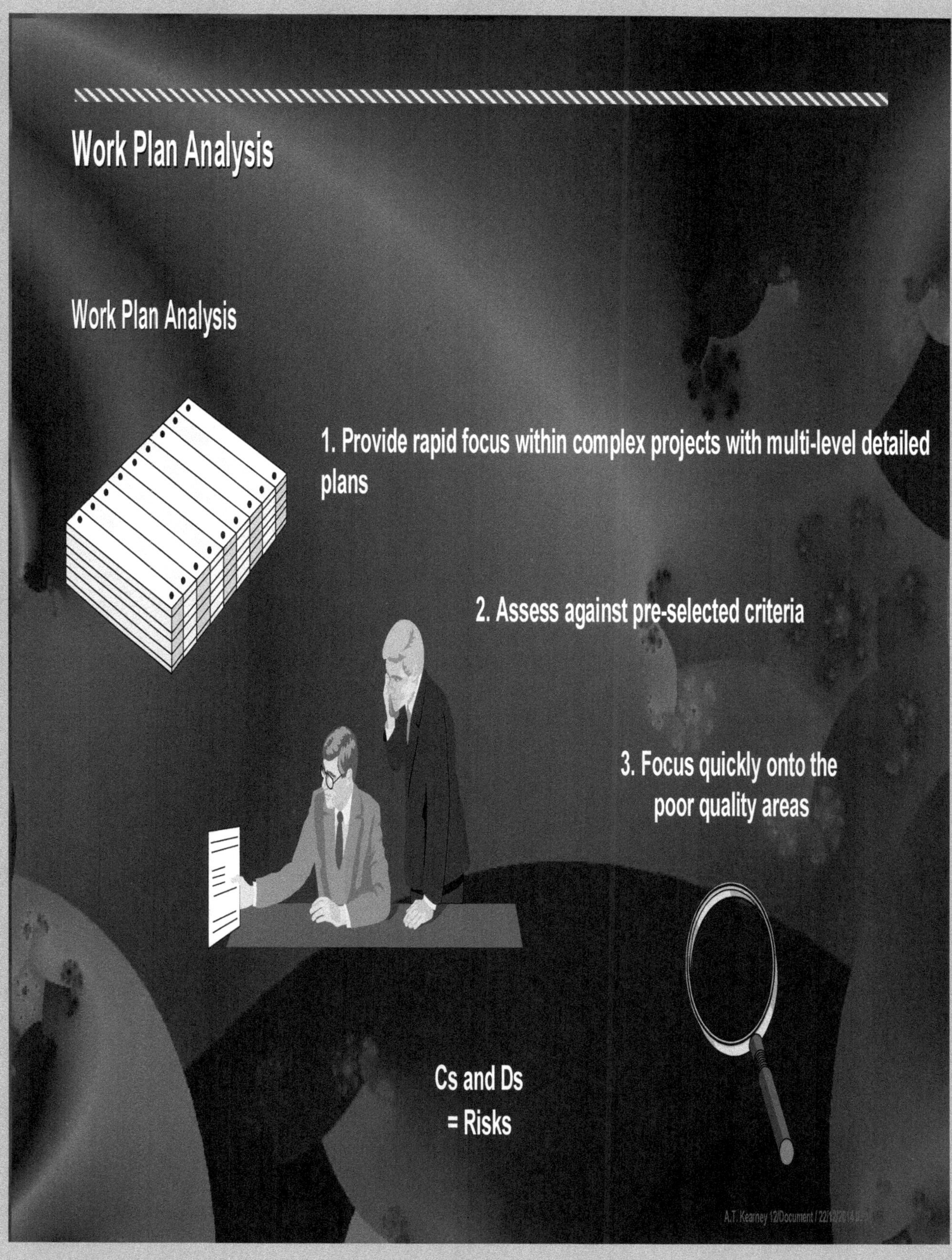
Work Plan Analysis
Work Plan Analysis
1. Provide rapid focus within complex projects with multi-level detailed plans
2. Assess against pre-selected criteria
3. Focus quickly onto the poor quality areas
Cs and Ds
= Risks

Change identification
Work Plan Analysis
Project Readiness Walkthroughs
Plan Hot-Spot analysis
Timescale Change Analysis
Health Check Diagnostic using pre-selected assumptions

Work Plan Analysis

Pre-selected assumptions - Example

- 1. Create the case for change
  - All critical benefits identified in the business case will prove realistic and be achieved
- 2. Manage the programme
  - The current governance structure, processes and plans will prove adequate to successfully deliver the programme
- 3. Align, engage and mobilise leadership
  - Senior management and project sponsors will continue to be committed to, engaged with all key aspects of the programme
- 4. Align, engage and mobilise organisation ....

A.T. Kearney 12/Document / 22/

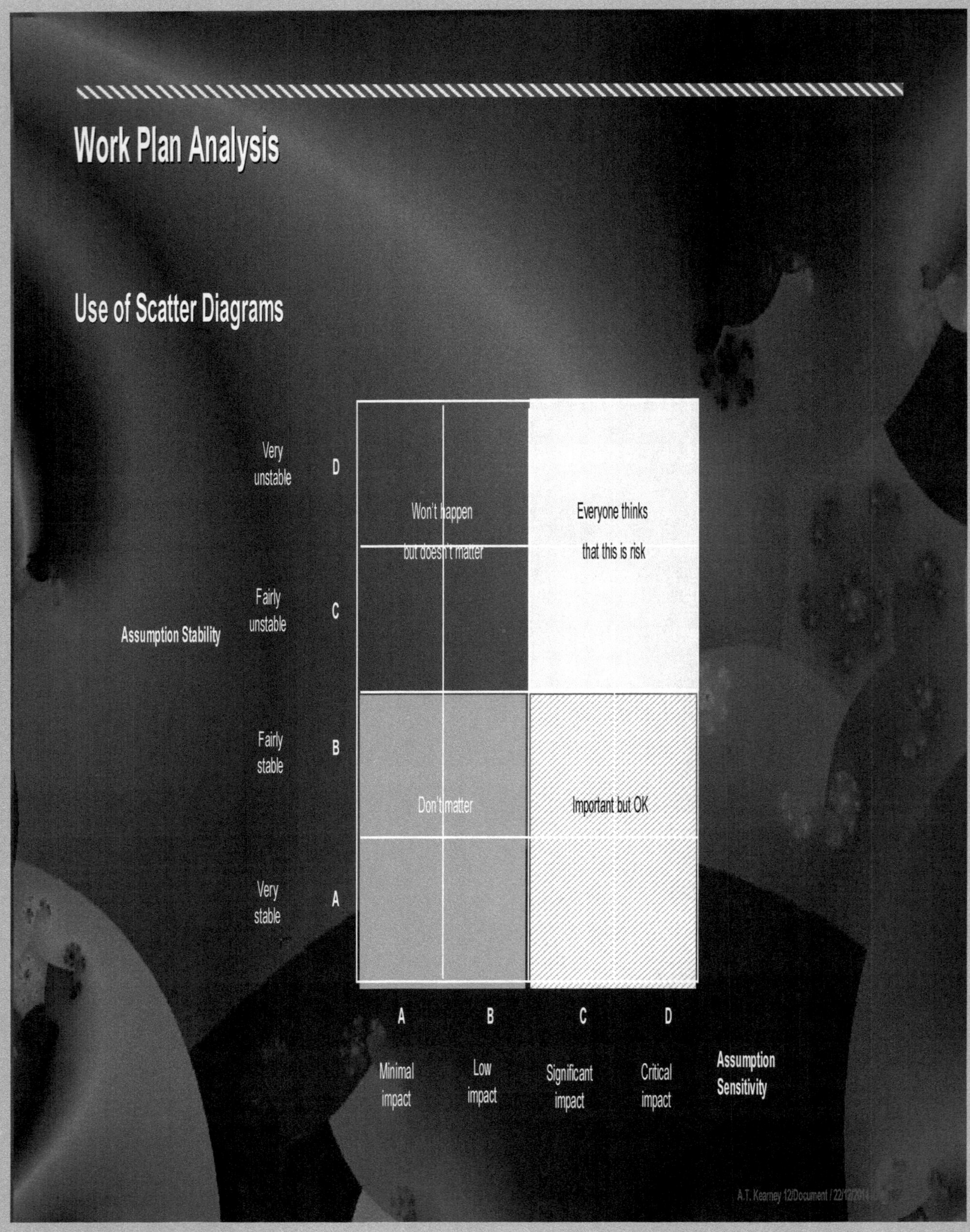
Work Plan Analysis
Use of Scatter Diagrams
Very unstable
D
Fairly unstable
C
Assumption Stability
Fairly stable
B
Very stable
A
Won't happen
but doesn't matter
Everyone thinks
that this is risk
Don't matter
Important but OK
A
B
C
D
Minimal impact
Low impact
Significant impact
Critical impact
Assumption Sensitivity

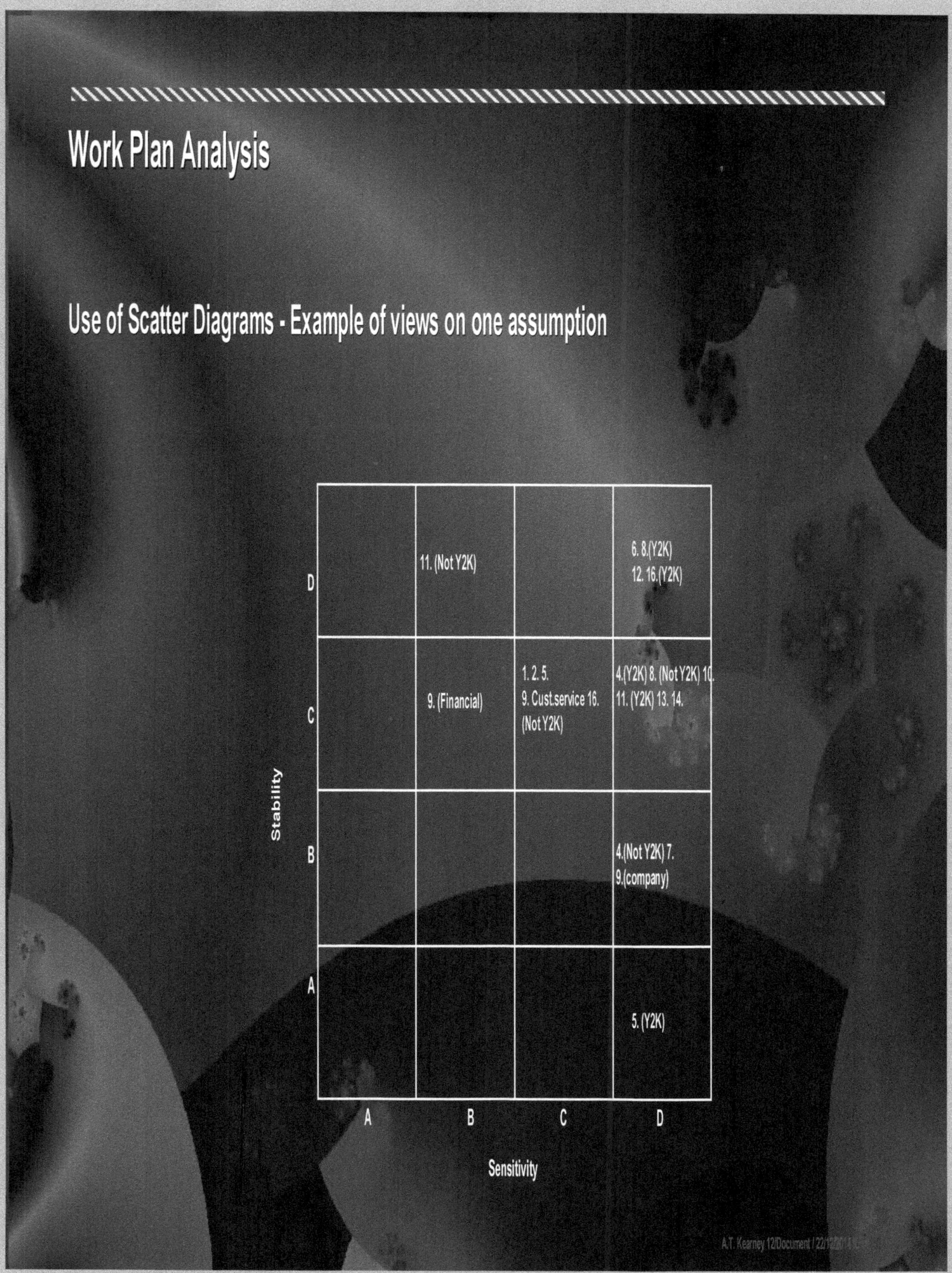
Work Plan Analysis
Use of Scatter Diagrams - Example of views on one assumption
11. (Not Y2K)
6. 8.(Y2K)
12. 16.(Y2K)
9. (Financial)
1. 2. 5.
9. Cust.service 16.
(Not Y2K)
4.(Y2K) 8. (Not Y2K) 10.
11. (Y2K) 13. 14.
4.(Not Y2K) 7.
9.(company)
5. (Y2K)
Stability
D
C
B
A
A
B
C
D
Sensitivity

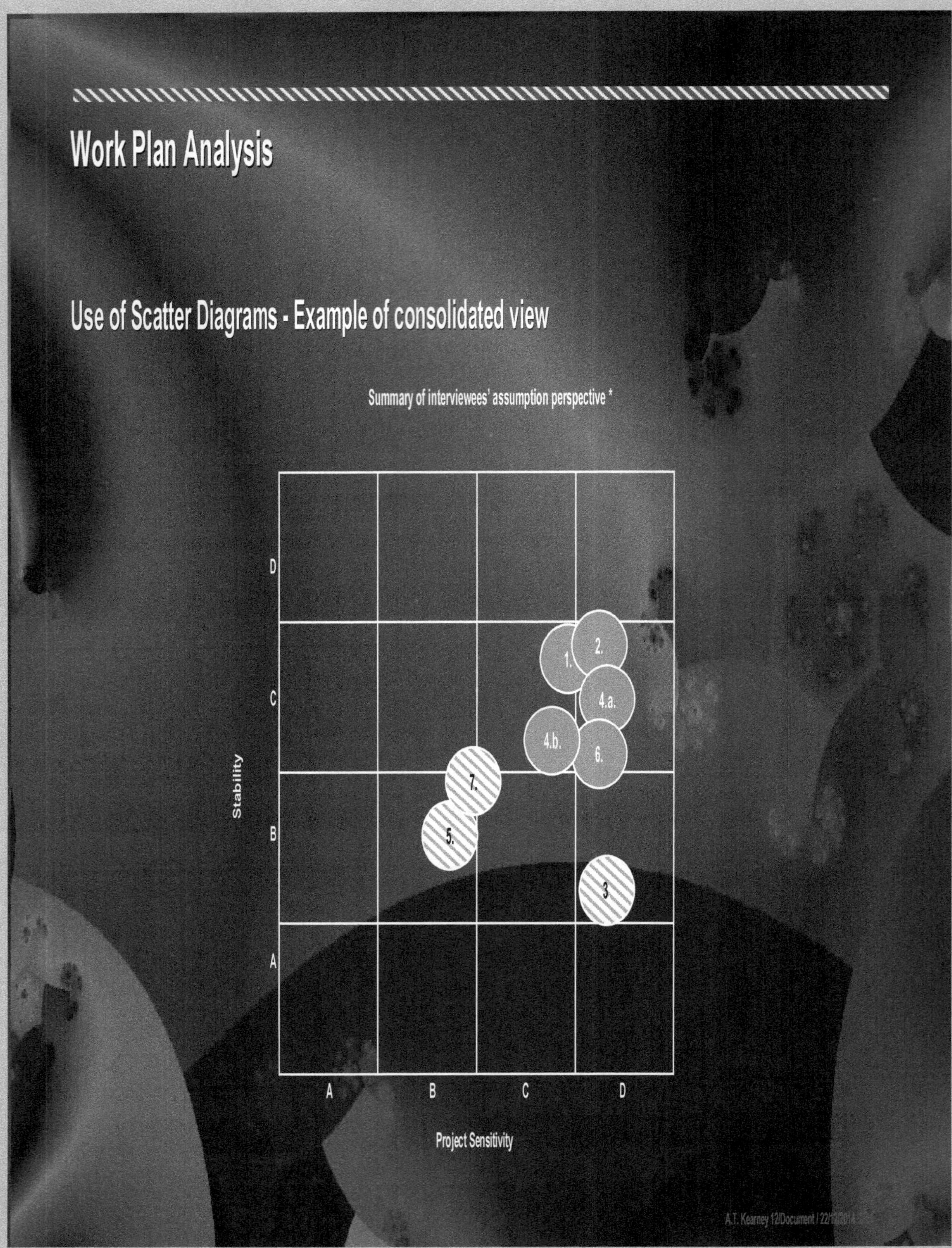
Work Plan Analysis
Use of Scatter Diagrams - Example of consolidated view
Summary of interviewees' assumption perspective *
Stability
D
C
B
A
1.
2.
4.a.
4.b.
6.
7.
5.
3
A
B
C
D
Project Sensitivity
A.T. Kearney 12/Document

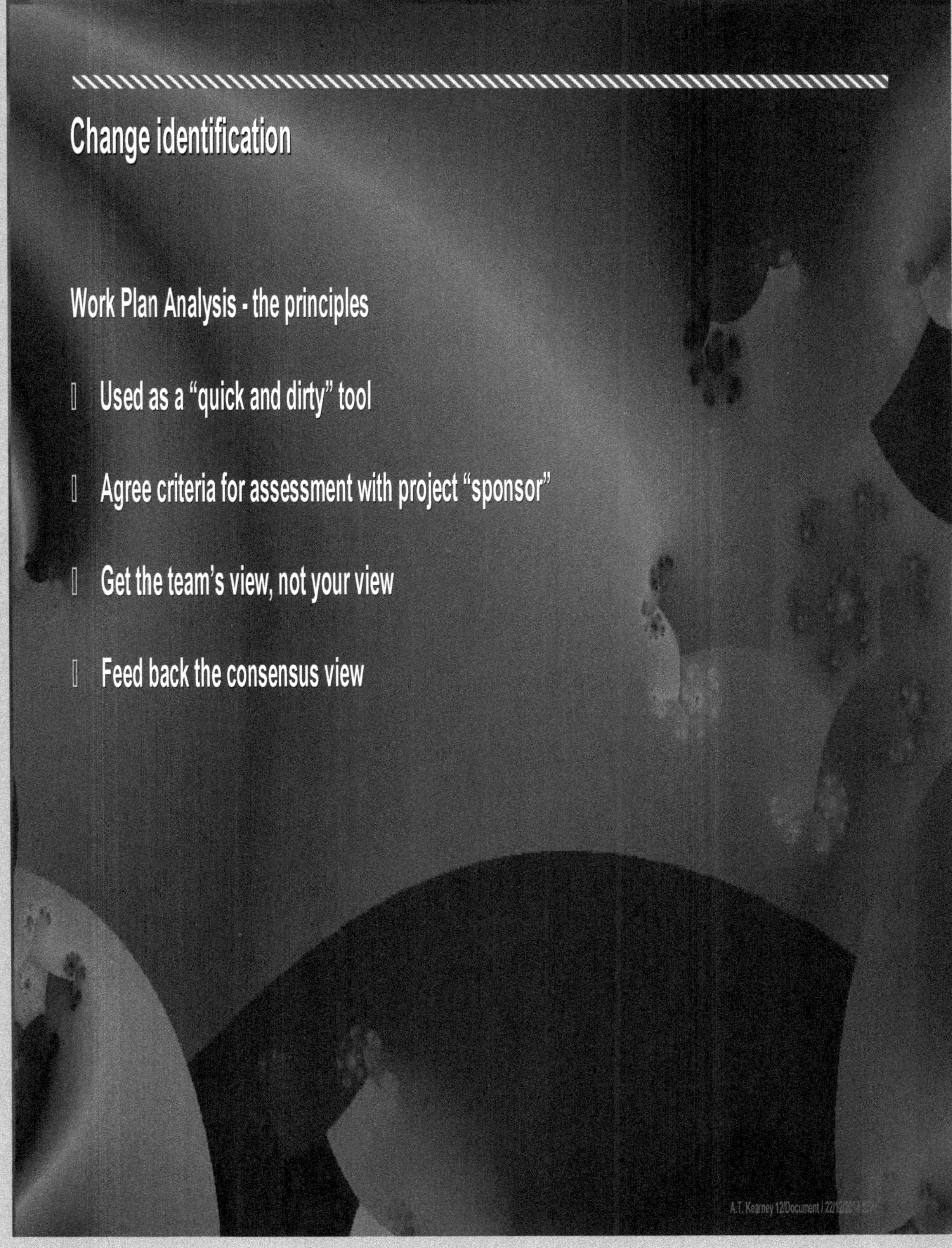
Change identification
Work Plan Analysis - the principles
Used as a "quick and dirty" tool
Agree criteria for assessment with project "sponsor"
Get the team's view, not your view
Feed back the consensus view

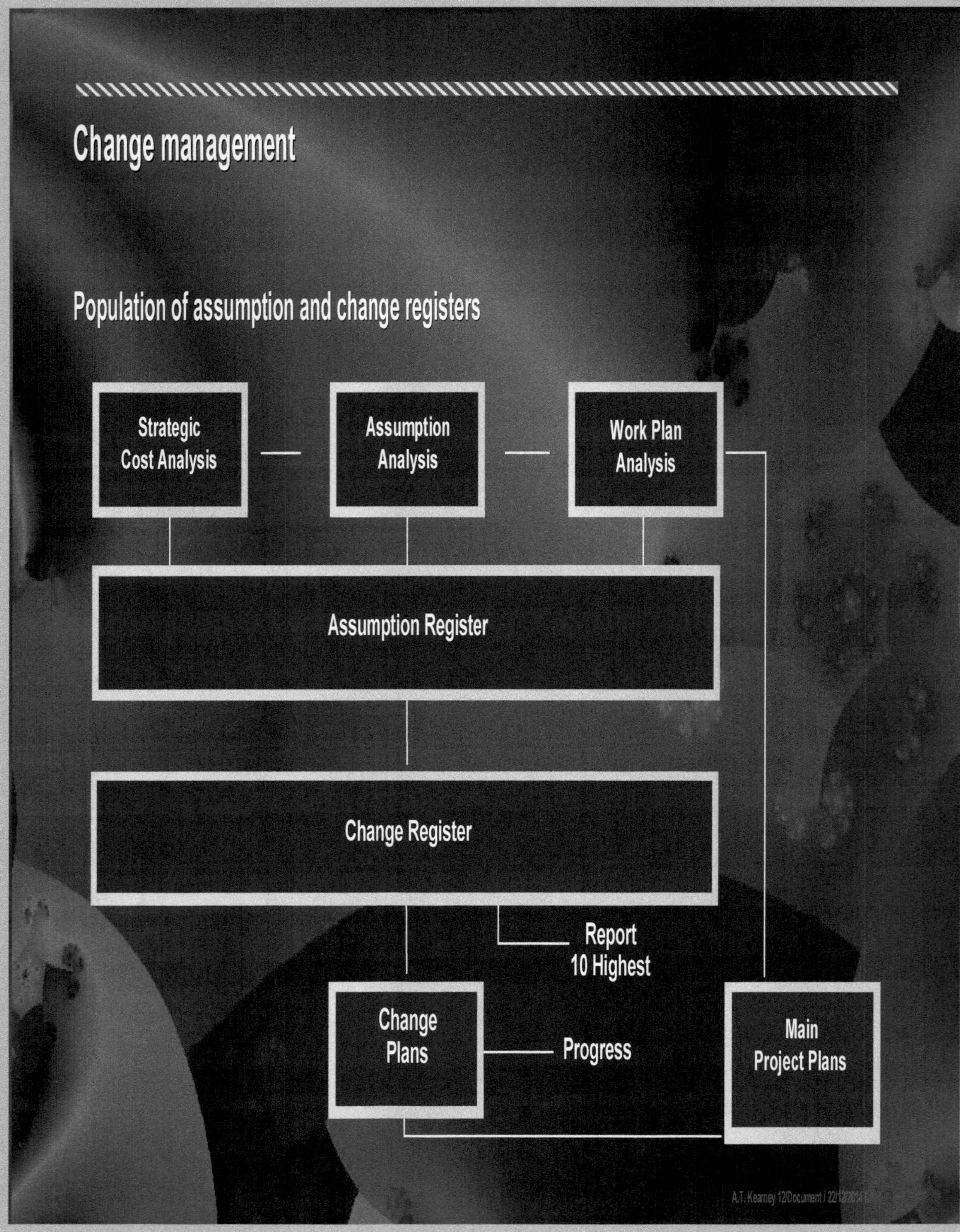
Change management
Population of assumption and change registers
Strategic Cost Analysis
Assumption Analysis
Work Plan Analysis
Assumption Register
Change Register
Report 10 Highest
Change Plans
Progress
Main Project Plans

SECTION THREE

6. IMPLEMENTATION OF STRATEGY

6.1 SUCCESS AND FAILURE

The success, or failure, surrounding a Change Management Strategy depends almost entirely on people, those who are designing and developing it and those who are expected to implement it. If the system is designed in such a way as to be too complicated to understand and comply with, or in such a way that makes it almost impossible to do ones job, then it would be rejected by those who should implement it.

Implementation of the policy is likely to involve modification of employment contracts. Monitoring the passage of information in and out of the organisation will involve human communication as well as technological means of communicating, such as the analysis of e-mails sent by employees, which can infringe their human rights, as can monitoring which sites are accessed on the Internet.

Care in selecting those who implement the Change Management principles can substantially influence the level of confidence attained. The programmes require parameters to be set and therefore the level of understanding of your business requirements and the software will influence policies success or otherwise.

The communication exercise to the employees is probably the most important part of the implementation. If left to the I.T. department, it may be delivered in seem-technical language or in terms of the needs of the business, rather than in terms and language to which employees can relate. Failure to allocate sufficient budgets to this area can put the success of a change management policy in jeopardy. It is also important to remember to include training in this area as part of the employees' induction.

Adoption of a Code of Ethics can be a useful adjunct to the process, as can the use of an external communication company.

6.2 PROGRAMME OBJECTIVES

It is a fact that most large, complex projects and programs fail to meet their planned objectives and as a consequence, most organisations are undertaking one or more aggressive programs at any point in time. These may fundamentally change the way the company conducts its business and failure to meet objectives on time may lead to a catastrophic loss of business.

Some projects or programmes can be chaotic at times. Objectives are evolving and plans and priorities are constantly changing. There is a temptation to accept this chaos as a necessary 'nature of the beast'. However, it is essential to move the programme forward in a traditional project management way by making sure that objectives and plans move forward.

Once we have clear objectives and plans, programme managers must control two fundamental factors if they are to be successful:

- **The business plan must be clearly identified,**
- **The implementation of the program must be made explicit.**

This can be answered by isolating the fundamental cause of most, if not all-major project problems. It can be argued that projects only fail due to two fundamental reasons:

- **The plans are proven to be incorrect,**
- **The significance of these plans is misunderstood.**

The capture, analysis, and communication of such assessments are, therefore, critical to the success of any project. This forms the basis of the Change Management method.

This method has been applied by PsySys Limited to help many diverse organisations to deliver large, complex projects and programmes on time, to budget and in meeting the expectations of demanding users.

6.3 Suggested Method

The focus of the method is based on the capture and analysis of the critical events and their assessments within the project plans, processes, and procedures.

The method is essentially a framework process that allows the capture of collective knowledge and viewpoints from those involved on the project, in a form that facilitates communication of events, assessments and ensures the pro-active management of changes. This is accomplished by dramatically improving communications, risks (which may be caused by changes) are avoided or managed to the optimum, and project objectives are delivered on time.

In essence, this is the mechanism by which the functions of programmes and projects are held together as a result of the principles operating within the method.

This, in effect, includes the varied events, their assessments, and the consequential changes relating to or consisting of a system. Methodical in procedures and plans, these are addressed to those involved and deliberating within the parameters of their systems development responsibilities.

The results being dependable on the mutual or reciprocal action which encourages those involved in the programmes and projects to communicate with each other and to work closely with a view to solving the threatening events before they impact on the development of the system.

The individuals involved maintain an approach, which relates and characterises the whole group of those involved in assessing the events and attacking the threatening ones before any changes become risks to the development of the system.

Following the system architects and the change management practitioners enables this. Simply follow the approved body of systems development methods, rules and management procedures employed by their organisation. For practical or even ethical reasons, it must be noted that with such a philosophy, it is seldom possible to fulfil all requirements of very large organisational systems.

As such, the suggested method is administered in the various applications. Putting to use such techniques and in applying the change management principles in the development of various applications will involve numerous and varied activities. A concrete issue in developing new applications is the problem of communication among the people involved, the motivation constantly needed for generic work, the ability to interact systematically and in using a structured systems methodology.

6.4 Features and Benefits of the Approach

The key features and benefits of the PsySys Limited approach are:

- ***Communication* — provides a simple, common, language for the communication of risk up, down and sideways within the organisation, whilst avoiding the normal problems of political sensitivity and risk aversion.**

- ***Control* — enhances project control by exception management and achieves an overview of change at senior management levels.**

- ***Information* — encourages the sharing of change information, establishing common objectives, discouraging change transfer and hence reducing the overall risk to all involved parties.**

- ***Flexible* — an adaptable process, which is rigorously applied to ensure that all significant changes are identified and controlled at the appropriate time.**

- ***Acceptable* — the non-intrusive/non-bureaucratic management process improves management discipline across the organization and is readily accepted by project teams.**

7. ASSESSMENT ANALYSIS

7.1 STRUCTURED TECHNIQUES

The core of *Change* is in the Assessment Analysis. This uses structured techniques to analyse project plans and identify the most sensitive events that are potentially unstable, and therefore the source of greatest change.

Everything is rated on a GAR principle: *G*reen, *A*mber and *R*ed scale; where G is always "good" and R is always "bad". This provides an instantly understood assessment on each stage: Events, Assessments, and Changes in relationship with the time scales as used in the plans. This, effectively, provides guidance on how best to handle the change.

7.2 STRATEGIC COST ANALYSIS

Costing is a process within the approach that can be used to define the cost of a requested change within a project or business area from as early as the proposal stage. It works by adding a 'quality' dimension to the estimating process so that high quality estimates, based on relevant experience, are treated differently from low quality estimates, which are little more than guesses.

The output takes the form of a probability distribution diagram and a set of assessments, which need to be managed in order to move the curve to the left and squeeze it (i.e. reduce the likely cost and the uncertainty).

Costing is particularly useful in the early stages of a project when the final cost of the project is subject to great uncertainty. The process has also been effectively used to define business budgets for re-structured business areas.

7.3 System Tool for Change Administration

A Microsoft Access based tool or any type of an ordinary spreadsheet can be utilised to allow the events, assessments, and changes to be captured and reviewed by all stockholders in the program. In this way changes that would have been missed are captured through the identification of events.

7.4 Work Plan Analysis

Work Plan Analysis is a set of techniques that enables a rapid change assessment to be undertaken on a complex project, which is already in progress.

It is always difficult to focus on the right areas when the project organisation is large and the plans are extensive and likely to be multi-levelled. Using Work Plan Analysis, the 'poor quality' areas of a project are quickly highlighted for further investigation.

One very successful application of this approach has been through the use of Project Readiness Assessment Walkthroughs. These are structured review meetings held just prior to major project milestones or deliverables. Initially the project team explain their self-evaluation of the project status and are questioned by an independent review team. Potential changes arising are captured using the Assessment Analysis process.

7.5 Communicating the Changes

The technique summarised above will only deliver its full benefits to any business if a suitable governance structure is quickly established to communicate the change information and set suitable actions to mitigate the changes. The mapping of the process onto an organisation is the key step to ensuring that the investment in the process is fully realised.

7.6 USING THE CONTENTS OF THIS BOOK

The level of treatment of the material in this book assumes that the reader has already understood the principles already explained. With this in mind, the author attempts to explain the:

- **Basic principles of change management and contrasts the more traditional approaches with the theories that underpin the thinking behind the process,**
- **Practicalities of launching a process into a new project and/or organisation,**
- **The process described includes some of the practical considerations of applying the popular approaches of Project Prioritisation and Assessment Analysis,**
- **Process of transferring ownership and embedding the method into the client's organisation.**

8. PRINCIPLES

8.1 Team Approach

An enterprise must escape from a culture based on transfer of changes between parties, to a team approach that is focused on implementing changes. Methods must be effective without the need for detailed time-consuming analysis.

8.2 Definition of a Change

A change may be perceived as a possible loss. A change is individual to a person or organisation because another as a minor change may perceive what one individual as a major change perceives.

A change is linked very strongly with competitiveness. Each decision has the possibility of resulting in loss. Each decision to introduce a new product into the marketplace can result in varying degrees of loss or gain. To be entrepreneurial is to accept change, that is, the possibility of loss. A good entrepreneur's strength, however, is to make decisions which maximise possible gain. Hence minimise possible loss, which constitutes effective change management.

Change is inherent in all aspect of an organisation and may be viewed from four primary directions: financial, operational, programme/project and portfolio/products. Many changes are related to the running of the operations and its processes but are often in trying to change operations that the greatest change is experienced. It is the management of change in such 'change' projects that the method addresses.

A project can be described in its simplest terms as: Planning to achieve specific objectives and then executing the plans. The emphasis is on the word 'plan' as without a plan we have no project. So in the context of a project, a change is something, which might disrupt the plans such that the objectives of the project are not met. The discipline of Project Change Management is thus a framework of techniques, which allows the project manager to pro-actively identify and manage changes before they develop into problems, which will impact the project plans.

8.3 Approaches

In recent years we have seen large projects in many areas of business suffering from a lack of control. The size of cost and time over-runs do not seem to be decreasing, despite the amount of management time which is being dedicated to analysing and quantifying the potential problems and selecting suitable personnel and processes. One may conclude that management, either do not have the correct methods and tools in place to attack the potential problems, or that they are not using, or do not understand, those which they do have.

In the early 1970's, the concepts of formal project change management began to emerge. Hailed as the saviour of project managers, in practice the results have been mixed. Change management has proved highly effective in certain mature industries - e.g. the Petrochemical or construction industry where project managers can base their estimates on years of similar engineering experience. Difficulties seem to be encountered when these traditional Change Management methods are applied to innovative and fast evolving areas such as Information Technology.

8.4 Events and Change Registers

Most projects will have an Events Register and some may have what they call a Change Register. In effect, this tends to be a list into which anyone can input the concerns. It will contain references to current problems, questions, and assessments, difficult activities about which there is reasonable confidence and the odd real change.

In any large project the Events or Change Register quickly becomes swamped with items that require very different actions and many which do not require any action at all. All this leads to an inevitable loss of focus. Further, the content tends to be biased towards current problems rather than future potential problems.

8.5 Individual Interviews

One-on-one interviews can be an effective way of capturing changes. When management and peers do not inhibit people, they tend to be far more open about their concerns. Unfortunately, most use much unsophisticated approaches such as "what do you see as your changes?" or "what keeps you awake at night?" Thus, if the person is being interviewed is sensitive to discussing changes it may prevent the capture of any valuable information.

At best the changes captured will tend to lack structure, as they are not focused onto the future objectives that the project plans to achieve.

8.6 Group Brainstorming

This action can be a very effective technique for opening up a very complex situation. However, information can be subconsciously suppressed by peer pressure, which may bias the discussion on one area at the expense of the rest of the project. Inevitably the mass of information captured is often difficult to focus, prioritise, and allocate ownership.

In general, it should be remembered that the quality of the output is only as good as the quality of the input data.

8.7 Analyses and Quantification of Changes

Changes may be difficult to capture reliably and concisely but further problems are likely to be experienced when trying to analyse them. Virtually all approaches to change analysis are based on estimating the factored impact of the change. This exposure to change is a combination of the chance (probability) of an event happening and the consequences (impact) if it does occur i.e.:

- Change Exposure = Potential Impact x Probability of Occurrence

Fundamental problems arise when individuals are required to estimate, numerically, the impact and then predict (numerically) the probability. Estimates, which are often little more than guesses, result in a single point estimate of Change Exposure, which is then given undeserved credibility in the detailed analysis of the change and used as the basis for many major project decisions. Also, it is often the case that part of the change impact can be quantified but often not the major part. An example can be based on an attempt to quantify bad publicity, quality, and relationship.

Some processes add complexity by rating the impact of changes in terms of financial, time scales, quality, performance etc., which quickly become very tedious to maintain.

8.8 Control and Lack of Follow-through

Many change management systems fail due to a lack of follow-through on actions. There is a surprising tendency to identify changes and then watch them happen!

This is caused by:

- **Failure to use the change register to set appropriate action plans,**
- **Lack of regular updates/maintenance of the change register,**
- **Absence of named owners and deadlines (lack of ownership),**
- **Tracking generalities rather than specifics,**
- **Concentrating on what can be done if the change occurs rather than stopping the change happening (pro-active),**
- **Trying to transfer the change elsewhere, without considering the consequences.**

8.9 Transfer of Change

Change transfer often occurs because the partner who knows most about the level of change within the enterprise (i.e. the supplier/purchaser relationship) is encouraged to transfer this to the other partner. Once accomplished, the party with the most knowledge of the change relaxes and the most ignorant partner inherits the change. An example of this is the Purchaser insisting on a fixed-price contract in a poorly defined contract when they know that the supplier does not understand the scope of the contract.

The supplier then has a tendency to deliver the minimum possible and obtain sign-off for everything, irrespective of quality. The effect of this type of commercial 'table-tennis' is actually to increase the level of change within the enterprise as the real changes pile up without intervention.

What is needed is a method that identifies and encourages the attack of real change at source. Such a method would force projects within the enterprise to become pro-active by attacking risky changes, rather than waiting for events to unfold and then counting the cost, as recorded in the previous month's financial returns.

8.10. Project and Change Management

There is often a tendency to treat change management as no more than another necessary evil of project management. Thus, it often becomes an additional administrative burden for the Project Manager and consequently does not get the quality attention to make it work effectively.

In order to make change management work, a shift in philosophy is required. This must lead the project team to view the process not just as another component of project management, but more as the communication stabiliser that holds the project together.

8.11 RISK CYCLE

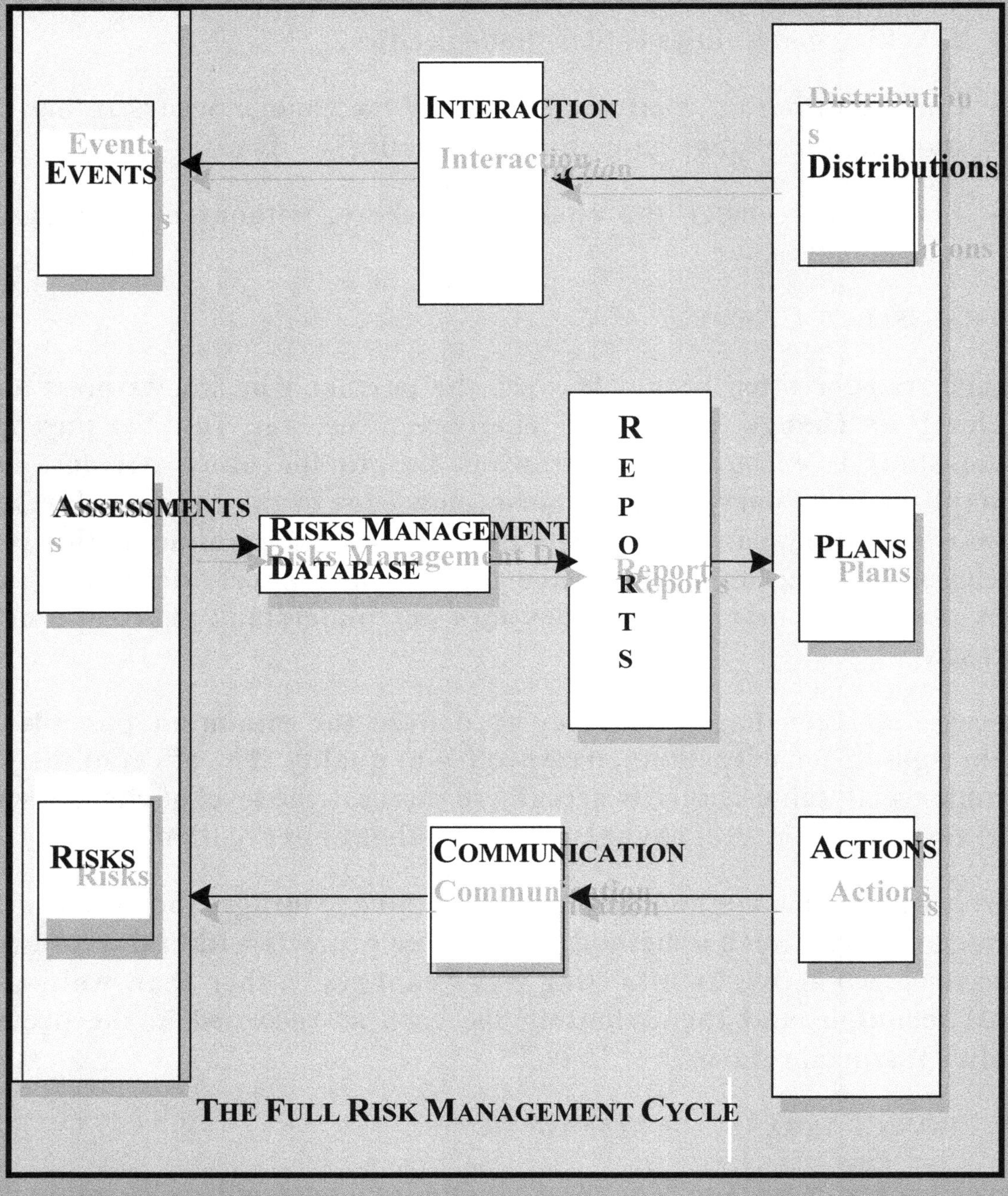

9. BASIC PRINCIPLES

9.1 Effective Means

The Process provides an effective means of managing changes within all types of projects. The process grew out of a thorough assessment of the problems often encountered in project management and the techniques of the traditional change management approaches that have been used to try and improve the situation.

Both good and bad principles were noted and new techniques were introduced to address key deficiencies. The resulting change management process has a proven track record of delivering tangible results in large projects across a diverse range of organisations.

9.2 Communication of Assessments

As already highlighted, a fundamental reason for project failure is the lack of quality communications both within the project and between the programme and its environment. Most problems incurred by projects could be avoided if information was effectively communicated in a timely fashion. The problem is that there is so much information that it is difficult to decide what needs to be communicated and to whom. This is where assessments come in.

Everything important associated with a project can be captured and tracked as an assessment:

- Activities are sized on the basis of assessments,
- Milestones are set according to assessments,
- Dependencies are based on assessments,
- Plans are executed by making assessments.

Therefore, the capture, analysis, and communication of assessments are critical to the success of any project, and this forms the core of the Project Change Management process.

9.3 Current Project Plan and Baseline

Capturing the critical assessments in the project plans are uncertain identifies changes. In other words, anything that might stop the objectives, time scales, and budget of the project plan being achieved. In this way, all assessments are effectively referenced to the project plans. Consequently, the plan provides the focus for the change management process.

This approach keeps the changes specific, forward looking and ensures that the plan is always sufficiently detailed and up to date.

9.4 Uncertainty Equals Risk in Changes

Risk in changing is inherent whenever there is uncertainty. The best judges of uncertainty are those who are asked to make estimates for the plans and, in most circumstances, the people who will actually have to do the work make the best estimators.

Combining this principle with the assessments captured from the project plans leads us to rate assessments for quality/uncertainty. Analysis is concentrated onto the areas of the project about which little is known and particularly the inter-dependencies that often represent the highest risk.

9.5 Judging the Quality Using the Scale

To capture this vital information about how sure the estimator is, each estimator is asked, not only for assessments or the value of any estimate, but also, what quality he or she considers the assessment or estimate to be. This is not a judgement of the skill of the estimator. It is a self-assessment of the current quality of the basic information, upon which the project plans are based.

The scale is defined for multiple uses throughout the process. It always means effectively the same thing i.e. 'A' is always good and 'C' is always bad. 'B' expresses tendencies to the two extremes.

- **A (Green) means very good, high confidence, not important**
- **B (Amber) means fairly good, reasonable confidence, not very important**
- **C (Red) means very poor, little or no confidence, and critically important.**

It should be noted that the method does not allow the estimator to say that the estimate or assessment is of average quality. The whole principle is that we should be forced to make a choice between good, high confidence and bad, low confidence estimates and cannot 'sit on the fence'.

Using these simple A, B, C terms to express degrees of uncertainty, it is possible to encourage the estimator to reveal a wide range of uncertainty. Also, it is often possible to persuade him or her to make estimates when not normally prepared to do so. Being able to qualify an assessment or estimate with a C quality, often assures the estimators that they will not be forced into a given value or statement. We can thus gain vital information about the uncertainty and therefore the risks if one goes ahead with a change that may lie at the heart of the project.

9.6 Process Overview

The process consists of an integrated closed loop method, which logically progresses through:

- Project Prioritisation (for multiple project environments),
- Change Assessment (consisting of Assessments Analysis plus Strategic Cost Analysis and/or Work Plan Analysis, if appropriate),
- Changes Prioritisation (to decide the 'order of attack'),
- Change Control (to put the mitigation plans into action and monitor their effectiveness).

9.7 Project Prioritisation

A large organisation may have, at any one time, hundreds of projects of varying sizes, and nature. Yet many organisations have no formal mechanism for prioritising projects leading to problems such as:

- Not knowing which projects should be approved/resourced,
- Uncertainty as to which projects should be formally assessed for Changes Assessment.

Once the critical and potentially changes to the projects have been identified, the book offers three change assessment techniques to identify and analyse the specific changes within each project.

The Assumption Analysis technique provides a backbone onto which the Strategic Cost Analysis and/or Work Plan Analysis approaches can be built.

In this respect Assumption Analysis would always be applied, Strategic Cost Analysis would be used in the early stages of a project or proposal to address the uncertainty in the cost/pricing of the project and Work Plan Analysis may be used to assess a very complex project which is well progressed.

9.8 Prioritisation of Changes

The specific changes captured from each project assessment needs to be prioritised in order to allocate resources and decide the order in which the risks should be addressed.

In this case provide a simple framework, which rates each change for Criticality, Controllability, and Impact Timing. The resulting list of changes is captured in a Microsoft Access Change Register (or any type of spreadsheet) and the changes can be summarised in a diagram, which provides an executive overview of the project change profile.

9.9 Control of Changes

The method suggested provides a framework for change control based on taking both strategic and tactical views of implementing changes. The strategic approach is achieved by applying trend analysis to the underlying assessments to identify any strong Change Drivers, which can be neutralised together.

Tactical approaches match the complexity of the change action plan to the complexity of the change to minimise bureaucracy for simple-to-manage changes, whilst maintaining the necessary formality for complex changes.

10. PROGRAMME CHANGES

10.1 Scope within the Programme

Once the Project has started, a project change management team manages all changes. If there are any changes, a proposed solution is constructed and sent to all relevant teams (internal and often external to the project) for impact assessment. If the change has limited impact and can be funded from existing authorised funds, the Project/Programme board or director can authorise the change. It is up to the Project/Programme board to decide that the change needs to be escalated, either as funding is required, or because of the impact it may have on other projects/programmes.

If the change is approved, it would be implemented and if the change is rejected, the change notification/details will reflect the reason it is rejected. This cycle of changes to Project/Programme scope is continued for each change that is required, until the implementation is complete.

10.2 Options

The purpose of this section is to identify and outline the main options available for Change Management. A recommended option will be developed further into a plan for how the proposed solution will be implemented. Each solution for managing change across the account can be characterised under the following four categories:

- **Governance: The method in which changes are approved. It is possible that a single change may require budget approval. It is usually Governance that causes the biggest delays in any process and not obtaining necessary sign off can be disastrous, hence getting the hierarchy and escalation processes right is essential.**

- **Culture: The way in which people work together. The ideal culture for changes to be managed effectively is a true partnership. Hence each option must strive to drive the teams to work together better.**

- **Process: The steps people take to manage change. This is a purist point of view, of what activities take place in order to manage a change from a concept to an implemented product. This would include standards for forms and communication guidelines.**

- **Tool: Whether there is one tool to support a single process, or a number of tools that interface well with each other, the right tool/s has to be developed to meet the established Process requirements.**

10.3 Uncertain Event

A change is an uncertain event, which may have an adverse effect on the project's objectives. Using the Change Management methodology should be very effective in the quest for identifying changes throughout the project lifecycle.

Remember, the Change Management methodology is:

- **Forward looking, investigating problems and how to deal with threats,**
- **A tool enabling communication, getting people at all levels to talk to each other and to interact,**
- **A no blame team culture, bringing concerns into the open where actions can be taken and plans put in place, in order to stop a change occurring.**

10.4 Management Qualities Required

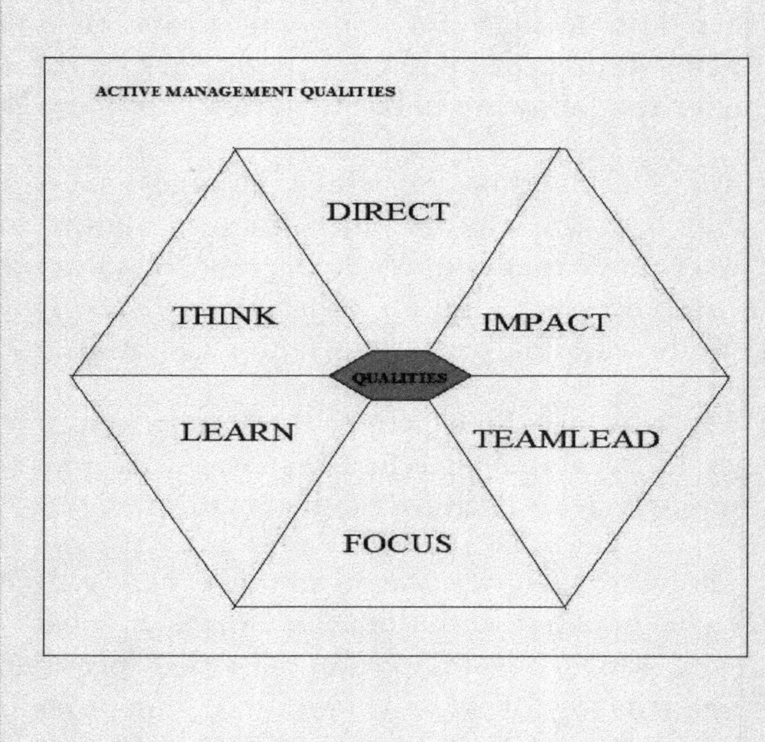

11. PROJECT SCORING

11.1 Score Graph

A scoring card graph can easily be produced on a spreadsheet and it could look something like this:

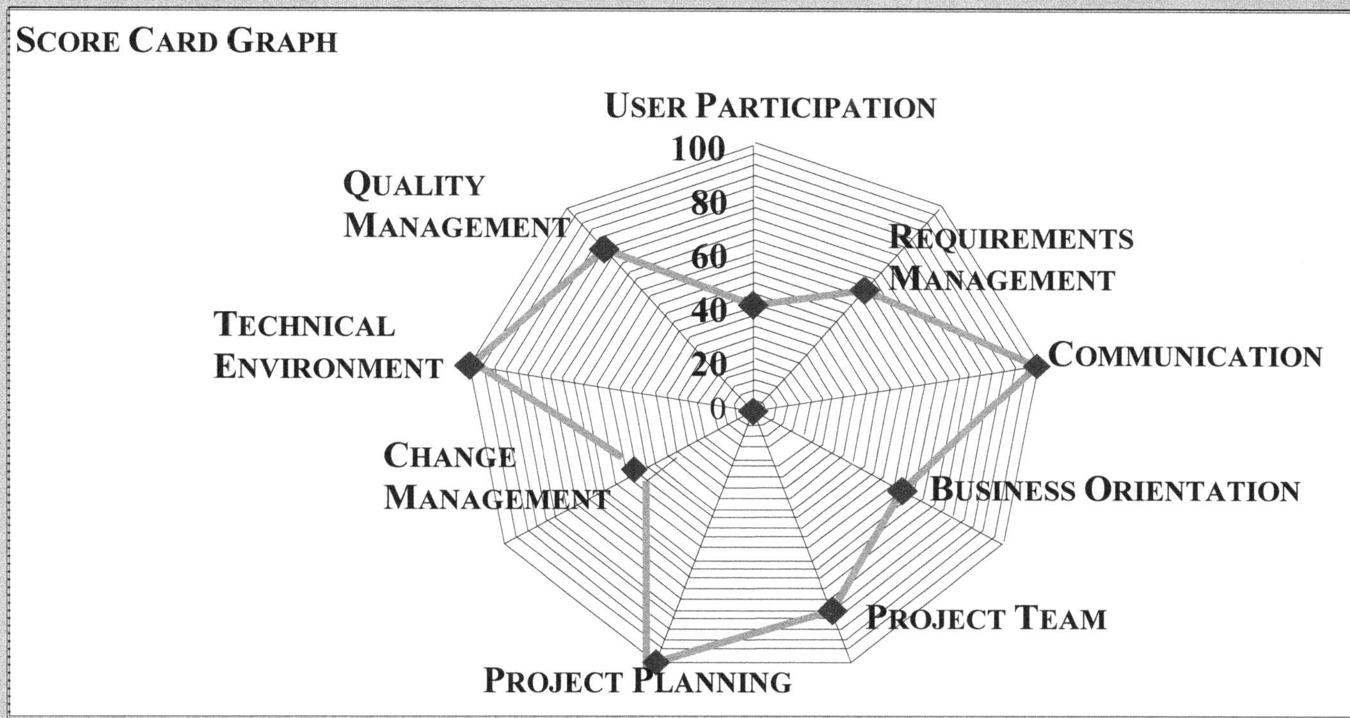

11.2 Scoring Points

1: USER PARTICIPATION	**17.5**		
Is there a clear focus on user involvement throughout project?			**0**
Does the project have representative users?			**0**
Is there a strong working relationship with the user?			**0**
Have all potential stakeholders been identified and engaged?			**0**
Project team & customer have agreed expectations for project?			**0**
2: REQUIREMENTS MANAGEMENT	**17.5**		
Is the project scope clearly defined, agreed, and reviewed regularly?			**0**
Clear, prioritized, & agreed written document of project requirements reviewed regularly?			**0**
Can prototypes be used to verify project requirements?			**0**
Mechanism for changes to requirements in place and actively being used?			**0**
Traceability of requirements against project deliverables?			**0**
3: COMMUNICATION	**15**		
Are regular status reviews held for whole project team?			**0**

Customer relationship maintained through regular communication?			**0**
Documented communication plan exists and is lived?			**0**
Effective internal & external reporting procedures?			**0**
Policy for team members to provide feedback?			**0**
4: BUSINESS ORIENTATION	**12.5**		
Do the project objectives align with the business strategy?			**0**
Does project have business case that details business benefits?			**0**
Can the business benefit be measured?			**0**
Does project team understand business domain?			**0**
Representation from all key areas of business impacted?			**0**
5: PROJECT TEAM	**10**		
Committed executive sponsor with necessary authority?			**0**
Shared common vision and common objectives?			**0**
Is there a sense of joint responsibility for ownership?			**0**
Does the project team have defined roles?			**0**
Does everyone in the team understand and perform their roles?			**0**
6: PROJECT PLANNING	**10**		

Detailed plans exist for project with clear visibility to user?		**0**
Project has schedule of small, regular, and attainable milestones?		**0**
Monitoring carried out against plan & communicated to users regularly?		**0**
Are timely actions being taken against deviations from the plan?		**0**
Is project management data being collected and used effectively?		**0**

7: CHANGE MANAGEMENT **7.5**

Up to date risk register logging all issues, assumptions, risks reviewed regularly?		**0**
Prioritized risks according to potential timeliness and impact?		**0**
Regular reviews of risk register involving whole project team and user?		**0**
Project has escalation pathway for dealing with potential risks?		**0**
Project has written plans for acting on potential & actual risks?		**0**

8: TECHNICAL ENVIRONMENT **5**

Project team has technical knowledge required to complete project?		**0**
Project manager has ability and time to manage project?		**0**
Project has access to correct development tools & tool knowledge?		**0**
Is training program in place to ensure required skills provided?		**0**

Supporting resources provided to ensure successful completion?		**0**
9: QUALITY MANAGEMENT	**5**	
Does agreed and documented quality plan exist and being lived?		**0**
Do practices & standards followed adhere to quality plan?		**0**
Is non-functional quality attributes required covered in quality plan?		**0**
Are deviations from standards & concessions documented?		**0**
Are internal work product reviews taking place?		**0**

OVERALL PROJECT STATUS:

Green: **80-100**

Amber: **61-79.5**

Red: **0-60.5**

11.3 Scoring Explanation

1. User Participation
The project has a responsibility to involve the user from conception through to delivery and beyond. This helps reduce the opportunity for misunderstandings, assists in the management of expectations, and promotes a collaborative approach to development.
Not only must the project involve users, but it must ensure that the users are representative of the whole user population. Different departments have different needs as do different job functions within those departments.
There must be a healthy and co-operative relationship between the user and the development team. This can be encouraged through two way communications on a regular basis, both formally and informally.
Whilst user involvement is critical, there will be other parties with a vested interest in the outcome of a project. These parties need to be identified and kept in touch with project progress.
By maintaining open lines of communication with the user the project can be spared the shock of unpleasant surprises when milestones are missed, and expensive and unnecessary rework can be avoided early on.
2. Requirements Management
One of the quickest ways for a project to spiral out of control is failure to agree and document the scope of the

project and its business objectives.
Requirements must be documented and prioritized with the agreement of the user and the development team. Requirements must be accurate, realistic, and unambiguous. Also, stated at the right level of detail as demanded by the stage of the project.
Functional or usability prototypes are an ideal method for verifying requirements and are relatively inexpensive to build. If prototypes are used, their use must be carefully managed along with user expectations. A prototype is not a complete system.
Change Control mechanisms and a Change Control Board with both user and project representatives must be in place before requirements changes can be made.
All requirements should be traceable from the original objectives through to the project deliverables. Traceability must be bi-directional. This ensures that all customer requirements have been met.
3. COMMUNICATION
The whole project team should be kept informed about the progress and status of the whole project throughout the development lifecycle. This encourages teamwork and ownership in the project as a whole.
Unless the communication line between the user and the project team remains open it is impossible for the team to manage the expectations of the user, and the team will lose valuable feedback from the user.
A clear communications plan assures both user and project team of their commitment to communicate with

each other in a timely and regular manner.
Project managers need to ensure that correct and accurate information is flowing through to all affected parties in a timely fashion. Informed team members are more effective than uninformed ones.
There must be an active policy to allow any member of the project team to escalate project issues and concerns either in person or anonymously to the appropriate level of management.
4. BUSINESS ORIENTATION
Projects are started to fulfill specific business needs which address the overall strategic aims of the business. Embarking on projects which are beyond the organization's experience is likely to be inherently risky.
IT projects are there to serve specific business needs and a documented business case within a value proposition is essential elements for project success.
Appropriate measures must be in place to monitor the commercial benefit to the business. The metrics must be defined and a baseline set down to monitor against.
It is essential that at least some members of the IT project team have exposure to the problem domain to ensure that project staff and customers understand a common language
IT projects often have to serve diverse business needs simultaneously and all impacted business areas must be represented as stakeholders in the project.

5. PROJECT TEAM
Projects need an individual, who has recognized standing within the organization, to act as the project champion and to assist in removing obstacles that impact on the project's chance of success.
There must be a common vision and understanding of the project objectives. Hidden agendas lead to conflict between members of the team and jeopardize the project as a whole
All members of the team need to feel that they have shared ownership of the project. This instills a sense of responsibility and commitment, and an inherent desire to perform at the highest level.
The project team needs clear definitions of roles and responsibilities ; e.g. Risk Manager, Configuration Manager etc.
Team members must have clear understanding of their own responsibilities but also other team member's responsibilities and the interfaces through which they must communicate.
6. PROJECT PLANNING
Projects need clear and visible schedules for their delivery commitments which are agreed with the customer, senior management, and the project team. Regular and early delivery reduces the risk of misunderstandings.
A project that commits to unrealistic and unattainable schedules will fail. Small and regular milestones help to

keep a project on track and maintain customer confidence.
It is not in the interest of the customer or the project to conceal problems and regular customer facing progress reports must be produced.
If a project is facing problems in keeping to its plans, actions must be assigned to individuals on the project team and escalated to the appropriate level of management at the earliest opportunity.
The project must ensure that project metrics are maintained to assist in planning and estimation both for the project itself and future projects.
7. CHANGE MANAGEMENT
A risk register is a dynamic tool used to document everything that has a potential negative effect on the project. The account recommends the used of the ABCD method of risk analysis.
All items recorded in the risk register must be prioritized and estimates made of size, likelihood and timing of their impact on the project.
The risk register must be maintained throughout the life of the project and must be visible to all members of the project team. Ownership of the risk register will usually reside with the project manager or a nominated risk manager.
The project must ensure that plans are in place to prevent risks happening or to reduce their effect if they cannot be prevented. Risk plans must be regularly

reviewed and executed in a timely manner if necessary.
It is understood that project teams will not always have the authority to execute their risk plans, and must ensure that appropriate lines of escalation are in place to take action. It is not usually good policy to transfer risk to other parties.
8. TECHNICAL ENVIRONMENT
A certain amount of project work can be learnt "on the job", but a project team must have a core number of people with the requisite technical knowledge to ensure that the team functions efficiently at the outset.
A project is likely to fail unless it has committed IT and User project manager's adequate time and ability to fulfill their roles.
Project team members must be provided with the appropriate development environment and the right tools to enable them to function at an optimum level, e.g. Configuration Management tools,
Training requirements must be identified early and incorporated into the project schedule. Training plans should be timed so that skills can be deployed as soon as possible after they are learnt.
Projects need supporting facilities to function correctly, e.g. real estate, administrative functions, hardware, etc. Resource acquisition must be executed as the project requirements demands.

9. QUALITY MANAGEMENT
The "Quality Plan" is a single document or set of documents that describes the measures that the project team will undertake to ensure that a satisfactory level of quality is maintained.
The project team must document its standards and practices in the Quality plan, and must ensure that these are being adhered to. Failure to observe documented practice may lead to withdrawal of ISO 9000 certification.
For software development projects it is vital to ensure that service oriented (non-functional) quality attributes such as performance, reliability are documented in the quality plan
It is recognized that projects may have to deviate from the QMS for specific reasons, but it is important that any deviations and their associated concessions are documented in the quality plan.
The Account is mandated to put all deliverable work products through peer review to maximize their value to the customer and to provide a learning experience for members of the project team.

SUMMING UP: TRAINING FOR CHANGES IN I.T.

This book, which is based on various consultancy assignments, considers detailed recommendations, including strategic changes, training, and the development of workshops. The reader, therefore, must consider such points that absorb resources, excessive costs and the incurrence of a heavy workload for existing staff.

Change Management and the changes to Configuration, Release, and Assets as a whole group of activities have traditionally been concerned with finding effective solutions to specific operational problems. The purpose of this book is to look at current problems and new, better methods, techniques, and tools for processing changes.

In the past, it has been found that some solutions are not implemented and, of those which are, too few survive the inclination to return to familiar ways of doing things. Change Management personnel have gradually come to realise that their tasks should include the solution of specific problems and the implementation of systems that predict and prevent future problems.

INDEX:

ALPHABETICALLY SEQUENCED CHAPTERS Page

BIBLIOGRAPHY

ALL BOOKS LISTED BELOW ARE WRITTEN BY THE AUTHOR, ANDREAS SOFRONIOU.

INFORMATION TECHNOLOGY AND MANAGEMENT

1. I.T. RISK MANAGEMENT, ISBN: 978-1-4467-5653-9
2. SYSTEMS ENGINEERING, ISBN: 978-1-4477-7553-9
3. BUSINESS INFORMATION SYSTEMS, CONCEPTS AND EXAMPLES, ISBN: 978-1-4092-7338-7
4. A GUIDE TO INFORMATION TECHNOLOGY, ISBN: 978-1-4092-7608-1
5. CHANGE MANAGEMENT IN I.T., ISBN: 978-1-4092-7712-5
6. FRONT-END DESIGN AND DEVELOPMENT FOR SYSTEMS APPLICATIONS, ISBN: 978-1-4092-7588-6
7. I.T RISK MANAGEMENT, ISBN: 978-1-4092-7488-9
8. I.T. RISK MANAGEMENT – 2011 EDITION, ISBN: 978-1-4467- *5653-9*
9. THE SIMPLIFIED PROCEDURES FOR I.T. PROJECTS DEVELOPMENT, ISBN: 978-1-4092-7562-6
10. THE SIGMA METHODOLOGY FOR RISK MANAGEMENT IN SYSTEMS DEVELOPMENT, ISBN: 978-1-4092-7690-6
11. TRADING ON THE INTERNET IN THE YEAR 2000 AND BEYOND, ISBN: 978-1-4092- 7577
12. STRUCTURED SYSTEMS METHODOLOGY, ISBN: 978-1-4477-6610-0
13. INFORMATION TECHNOLOGY LOGICAL ANALYSIS, ISBN: 978-1-4717-1688-1
14. I.T. RISKS LOGICAL ANALYSIS, ISBN: 978-1-4717-1957-8
15. I.T. CHANGES LOGICAL ANALYSIS, ISBN: 978-1-4717-2288-2
16. LOGICAL ANALYSIS OF SYSTEMS, RISKS , CHANGES, ISBN: 978-1-4717-2294-3
17. COMPUTING, A PRÉCIS ON SYSTEMS, SOFTWARE AND HARDWARE, ISBN: 978-1-2910-5102-5
18. MANAGE THAT I.T. PROJECT, ISBN: 978-1-4717-5304-6
19. CHANGE MANAGEMENT, ISBN: 978-1-4457-6114-5
20. THE MANAGEMENT OF COMMERCIAL COMPUTING, ISBN: 978-1-4092-7550-3
21. PROGRAMME MANAGEMENT WORKSHOP, ISBN: 978-1-4092-7583-1
22. MANAGEMENT OF I.T. CHANGES, RISKS, WORKSHOPS, EPISTEMOLOGY, ISBN: 978-1-84753-147-6
23. THE PHILOSOPHICAL CONCEPTS OF MANAGEMENT THROUGH THE AGES, ISBN: 978-1-4092- 7554-1
24. THE MANAGEMENT OF PROJECTS, SYSTEMS, INTERNET, AND RISKS, ISBN: 978-1-4092-7464-3
25. HOW TO CONSTRUCT YOUR RESUMÊ, ISBN: 978-1-4092-7383-7
26. DEFINE THAT SYSTEM, ISBN: 978-1-291-15094-0
27. INFORMATION TECHNOLOGY WORKSHOP, ISBN: 978-1-291-16440-4
28. CHANGE MANAGEMENT IN SYSTEMS, ISBN: 978-1-4457-1099-0
29. SYSTEMS MANAGEMENT, ISBN: 978-1-4710-4907-1
30. TECHNOLOGY, A STUDY OF MECHANICAL ARTS AND APPLIED SCIENCES, ISBN: 978-1-291-58550-6
31. EXPERT SYSTEMS, KNOWLEDGE ENGINEERING FOR HUMAN REPLICATION, ISBN: 978-1-291- 59509-3
32. ARTIFICIAL INTELLIGENCE AND INFORMATION TECHNOLOGY, ISBN: 978-1-291-

60445-0
33. PROJECT MANAGEMENT PROCEDURES FOR SYSTEMS DEVELOPMENT, ISBN: 978-0-952-72531-2
34. SURFING THE INTERNET, THEN, NOW, LATER. ISBN: 978-1--291-77653-9
35. ANALYTICAL DIAGRAMS FOR I.T. SYSTEMS, ISBN: 978-1-326-05786-2
36. INTEGRATION OF INFORMATION TECHNOLOGY, ISBN: 978-1-312-84303-1
37. TRAINING FOR CHANGES IN I.T. ISBN: 978-1-326-14325-1

MEDICINE AND PSYCHOLOGY

38. MEDICAL ETHICS THROUGH THE AGES, ISBN: 978-1-4092- 7468-1
39. MEDICAL ETHICS, FROM HIPPOCRATES TO THE 21ST CENTURY ISBN: 978-1-4457-1203-1
40. THE MISINTERPRETATION OF SIGMUND FREUD, ISBN: 978-1-4467-1659-5
41. JUNG'S PSYCHOTHERAPY: THE PSYCHOLOGICAL & MYTHOLOGICAL METHODS, ISBN: 978-1-4477-4740-6
42. FREUDIAN ANALYSIS & JUNGIAN SYNTHESIS, ISBN: 978-1-4477-5996-6
43. ADLER'S INDIVIDUAL PSYCHOLOGY AND RELATED METHODS, ISBN: 978-1-291-85951-5
44. ADLERIAN INDIVIDUALISM , JUNGIAN SYNTHESIS, FREUDIAN ANALYSIS, ISBN: 978-1-291-85937-9
45. PSYCHOTHERAPY, CONCEPTS OF TREATMENT, ISBN: 978-1-291-50178-0
46. PSYCHOLOGY, CONCEPTS OF BEHAVIOUR, ISBN: 978-1-291-47573-9
47. PHILOSOPHY FOR HUMAN BEHAVIOUR, ISBN: 978-1-291-12707-2
48. SEX, AN EXPLORATION OF SEXUALITY, EROS AND LOVE, ISBN: 978-1-291-56931-5
49. PSYCHOLOGY FROM CONCEPTION TO SENILITY, ISBN: 978-1-4092-7218-2
50. PSYCHOLOGY OF CHILD CULTURE, ISBN: 978-1-4092-7619-7
51. JOYFUL PARENTING, ISBN: 0 9527956 1 2
52. THE GUIDE TO A JOYFUL PARENTING, ISBN: 0 952 7956 1 2
53. THERAPEUTIC PHILOSOPHY FOR THE INDIVIDUAL AND THE STATE, ISBN: 978-1-4092-7586-2
54. PHILOSOPHIC COUNSELLING FOR PEOPLE AND THEIR GOVERNMENTS, ISBN: 978-1-4092-7400-1

PHILOSOPHY AND POLITICS

55. MORAL PHILOSOPHY, FROM SOCRATES TO THE 21ST AEON, ISBN: 978-1-4457-4618-0
56. MORAL PHILOSOPHY, FROM HIPPOCRATES TO THE 21ST AEON, ISBN: 978-1-84753-463-7
57. MORAL PHILOSOPHY, THE ETHICAL APPROACH THROUGH THE AGES, ISBN: 978-1-4092-7703-3
58. MORAL PHILOSOPHY, ISBN: 978-1-4478-5037-3
59. 2011 POLITICS, ORGANISATIONS, PSYCHOANALYSIS, POETRY, ISBN: 978-1-4467-2741-6
60. PLATO'S EPISTEMOLOGY, ISBN: 978-1-4716-6584-4
61. ARISTOTLE'S AETIOLOGY, ISBN: 978-1-4716-7861-5
62. MARXISM, SOCIALISM & COMMUNISM, ISBN: 978-1-4716-8236-0
63. MACHIAVELLI'S POLITICS & RELEVANT PHILOSOPHICAL CONCEPTS, ISBN: 978-1-4716-8629-0

64. **BRITISH PHILOSOPHERS, 16TH TO 18TH CENTURY, ISBN: 978-1-4717-1072-8**
65. **ROUSSEAU ON WILL AND MORALITY, ISBN: 978-1-4717-1070-4**
66. **EPISTEMOLOGY, ISBN: 978-1- 978-1-326-11380-3**
67. **HEGEL ON IDEALISM, KNOWLEDGE & REALITY, ISBN: 978-1-4717-0954-8**

SOCIAL SCIENCES AND PHILOLOGY

68. **PHILOLOGY, CONCEPTS OF EUROPEAN LITERATURE, ISBN: 978-1-291-49148-7**
69. **THREE MILLENNIA OF HELLENIC PHILOLOGY, ISBN: 978-1-291-49799-1**
70. **CYPRUS, PERMANENT DEPRIVATION OF FREEDOM, ISBN: 978-1-291-50833-8**
71. **SOCIOLOGY, CONCEPTS OF GROUP BEHAVIOUR, ISBN: 978-1-291-51888-7**
72. **SOCIAL SCIENCES, CONCEPTS OF BRANCHES AND RELATIONSHIPS ISBN: 978-1-291-52321-8**
73. **CONCEPTS OF SOCIAL SCIENTISTS AND GREAT THINKERS, ISBN: 978-1-291-53786-4**

FICTION AND POETRY

74. **THE TOWERING MISFEASANCE, ISBN: 978-1-4241-3652-0**
75. **DANCES IN THE MOUNTAINS – THE BEAUTY AND BRUTALITY, ISBN: 978-1-4092-7674-6**
76. **YUSUF'S ODYSSEY, ISBN: 978-1-291-33902-4**
77. **WILD AND FREE, ISBN: 978-1-4452-0747-6**
78. **HATCHED FREE, ISBN: 978-1-291-37668-5**
79. **THROUGH PRICKLY SHRUBS, ISBN: 978-1-4092-7439-1**
80. **BLOOMIN' SLUMS, ISBN: 978-1-291-37662-3**
81. **SPEEDBALL, ISBN: 978-1-4092-0521-0**
82. **SPIRALLING ADVERSARIES, ISBN: 978-1-291-35449-2**
83. **EXULTATION, ISBN: 978-1-4092-7483-4**
84. **FREAKY LANDS, ISBN: 978-1-4092-7603-6**
85. **SOFRONIOU COLLECTION OF FICTION BOOKS, ISBN: 978-1-326-07629-0**
86. **MAN AND HIS MULE, ISBN: 978-1-291-27090-7**
87. **LITTLE HUT BY THE SEA, ISBN: 978-1-4478-4066-4**
88. **THE SAME RIVER TWICE, ISBN: 978-1-4457-1576-6**
89. **THE CANE HILL EFFECT, ISBN: 978-1-4452-7636-6**
90. **WINDS OF CHANGE, ISBN: 978-1-4452-4036-7**
91. **A TOWN CALLED MORPHOU, ISBN: 978-1-4092-7611-1**
92. **EXPERIENCE MY BEFRIENDED IDEAL, ISBN: 978-1-4092-7463-6**
93. **CHIRP AND CHAT (POEMS FOR ALL), ISBN: 978-1-291-75055-3**
94. **POETIC NATTERING, ISBN: 978-1-291-75603-6**

www.ingramcontent.com/pod-product-compliance
Lightning Source LLC
Chambersburg PA
CBHW081226050326
40689CB00016B/3695